FABIAN SOCIETY

The Fabian Society is Britain's leading left of centre think tank and political society, committed to creating the political ideas and policy debates which can shape the future of progressive politics.

With over 300 Fabian MPs, MEPs, Peers, MSPs and AMs, the Society plays an unparalleled role in linking the ability to influence policy debates at the highest level with vigorous grassroots debate among our growing membership of over 7000 people, 70 local branches meeting regularly throughout Britain and a vibrant Young Fabian section, and the Fabian Women's Network. Fabian publications, events and ideas therefore reach and influence a wider audience than those of any comparable think tank. The Society is unique among think tanks in being a thriving, democratically-constituted membership organisation, affiliated to the Labour Party but organisationally and editorially independent.

For over 120 years Fabians have been central to every important renewal and revision of left of centre thinking. The Fabian commitment to open and participatory debate is as important today as ever before as we explore the ideas, politics and policies which will define the next generation of progressive politics in Britain, Europe and around the world.

Fabian Society
11 Dartmouth Street
London SW1H 9BN
www.fabians.org.uk

Fabian Ideas 629

First published 2011
ISBN 978 0 7163 0629 0

Series Editor and Editorial Director: Tom Hampson
Editorial Manager: Ed Wallis

Printed and bound by DG3, London, UK

To find out more about the Fabian Society, the Young
Fabians, the Fabian Women's Network and our local
societies, please visit our web site at **www.fabians.org.uk**.

The Credibility Deficit

How to rebuild Labour's economic reputation

Stephen Beer

About the author

Stephen Beer is senior fund manager with the Central Finance Board of the Methodist Church, where he is responsible for managing a UK Equity Fund run according to socially responsible investment criteria. He contributes economic and strategy analysis and also works with money market and bond funds.

He is chair of Vauxhall Constituency Labour Party and is the Christian Socialist Movement's political communications officer. He was a Labour parliamentary candidate in 2001.

The views expressed in this pamphlet represent Stephen Beer's personal opinion.

CONTENTS

Acknowledgements

A particular thank you to Tom Hampson for his support, work, and patience on this pamphlet, and Ed Wallis and Tim Horton for their work and input.

Thank you to both Fabian General Secretaries past and present, Sunder Katwala and his successor Andy Harrop, for helping to make it happen. Various people endured discussions with me on the theme over the past few months, including economists and strategists in the City and academia, for which much thanks.

Comments and questions from Nick Bent and Dan Gover were particularly helpful. Additional encouragement came from Andy Flannagan, director of the Christian Socialist Movement, and others. The conclusions and, of course, any errors, are mine.

- **Labour's economic credibility gap is wide but it can be closed.** Labour lost credibility on fiscal policy with financial markets and it lost credibility with the electorate because it did not provide answers to the concerns of people faced with declining living standards and little decline in inequality.

- During the crisis, Labour acted to protect bank deposits and the financial system. It changed its approach to intervention in the economy but the politics trailed what was happening. As a result Labour entered the General Election campaign **unable to explain its approach to the economy**.

- Labour should revisit its values, which are relevant to today's situation. **Values must not be crowded out of markets.** Everyone should be able to participate in our economic life and inequality works against this. Applying these values will require Labour to take some tough decisions.

- Deficits have a role to play in economic policy but there must be both **a clear plan for reducing large deficits** and controlling spending, and a significant plan to promote growth. Labour should combine this with an **'effective spending guarantee'** that it will retain tight control on spending.

- To restore credibility, Labour also needs to understand economic realities, including the power of the bond markets. **Stimulus measures should focus on investment** to raise the productive potential of the economy and, at the heart of what we are about, on employment, through measures similar to the Future Jobs Fund. Government should act as employer of last resort. These measures should take precedence over other spending priorities.

- Industrial intervention has its place but the main focus of government economic intervention should be on **helping the economy to function more effectively for the many not the few**. We should act to reduce uncertainty, for example with a stable and simple business tax regime and by stepping in where there is market failure, for example with respect to climate change. Action can be taken to make investment easier and promote skills.

- **The financial sector needs reform.** Labour can do this by supporting – and learning to love – a reformed City with a refreshed reputation and understanding of the common good. Banking activities should be separated. The corporate pay controversy should be addressed. Responsible investing should be encouraged.

INTRODUCTION

Labour must convince voters that it is credible on the economy if it is serious about winning the next General Election. Winning all the other policy battles will amount to little unless we win the battle for economic policy. At the moment, the hope seems to be that events will vindicate Labour's last budget plans. Harsh spending cuts introduced by the Conservative-Liberal Democrat Government will, it is believed, hit economic growth and make it still harder for the Government to reduce the annual deficit and pay down public sector debt. When this becomes apparent, the electorate will reject George Osborne's austerity measures and automatically restore its faith in Labour's economic approach. This seems to be the general assumption. It is almost certainly wrong.

Labour's credibility problems go much deeper, and it cannot simply hope that the public will come to believe Labour was right all along. This should be no surprise because Labour did have to change its economic policy during the crisis, even if it did not lose its conviction that government has a vital role in economic management. Indeed, perhaps it is more accurate to say that Labour rediscovered this conviction and that it did so, and acted to prevent the financial system from melting down, is to its credit. Voters, now looking at the financial storms hitting the US and other European countries are unlikely to be persuaded by alternative strategies which ignore market risks. They might be persuaded by an alternative free from an ideological commitment to spending cuts for their own sake.

Labour did not cause the financial crisis, but it did happen on its watch; this inescapable fact cannot be ignored. Labour also took bold action to rescue the financial system from collapse, both here and around the world. This inescapable fact *is* being ignored. Much of the public now believes that we are responsible for bequeathing the country a large amount of debt that must now be dealt with. We might argue that people have believed the claims of the Tory spin machine but this does not alter the situation. If Labour had simply been outspun on economic policy despite getting everything right, that would have been bad enough. But Labour did not get everything right. Its reputation had been tarnished going into the financial crisis and though it did the right things during the crisis its stature on the economy was further diminished.

Labour's debates since the General Election around the 'Good Society' or 'Blue Labour' have had little to say on the broad macroeconomic issues of the day. For a start, values matter (what, after all, do people mean by a *good* society?). Britiain faces a crisis of values whether applied to banking, the economy, the media, or public order. The good news here is that people want to see a higher ethic of behaviour (even while realising no one is perfect). They might be receptive to a political party that can avoid moral lectures but is clear about how it would encourage a more virtuous society.

Labour can make real progress by recalling its core values on the economy while recognising that the economy is dynamic. Economic policy is not simply about pulling a few levers in government and watching growth take off or inequality destroyed. It is about creating the incentives and overall conditions for growth and for a more efficient and fair economy. The ethical socialist view of the economy, with its emphasis on greater and fairer participation in economic life, matches well with this dynamic approach to the economy. The statist approach is dead. But there is still a vital role for the state, working to prevent the undue accumulation of economic power.

What about Labour's record on reducing unemployment, on fighting inequality and keeping inflation and interest rates low? These are remarkable achievements. Moreover, during our time in office we raised the wages of the low paid, lifted hundreds of thousands of children out of poverty, and built new schools and hospitals. These things did not just happen of their own accord. Even Labour members can underplay these gains. In government we changed the terms of the debate on what government could and should do. The Tory/LibDem Government's cutbacks cannot completely reverse the progress we made.

There is a political opportunity here for Labour but economic credibility will not simply land in our lap.

Yet in the current environment, those gains get us little further than base camp up the mountain that must be climbed to restore faith in Labour on the economy.

This pamphlet was written during a summer in which financial markets have been remorseless in their targeting of economies perceived to have economic policies that are no longer credible. This is not only because investors are worried about debt levels, but because they fear growth is threatened too. The conventional wisdom has been to bring forward plans to cut debt levels, which ties in with the smaller state ideologies of some. This risks hitting growth especially if every country cuts together, rather than working together to stimulate demand as Ed Miliband has called for. More people are realising that to be credible on the economy you must have debt reduction plans that are convincing and a comprehensive plan to promote sustainable growth. The coalition has a debt reduction plan which has convinced many, despite taking risks with growth. It would like to have a growth plan that was equally convincing. Labour has yet to articulate its plans for deficit reduction or growth.

The Conservatives and Liberal Democrats have their own building credibility problem on the economy with a public more sceptical that they have the answers. The coalition lead on the economy is fragile. There is a political opportunity here for Labour but economic credibility will not simply land in our lap. The public may believe spending cuts go too far but it still believes Labour made them necessary.

In this pamphlet I examine in more detail what Labour's credibility deficit looks like and how it came about. After exploring the impact of the financial crisis and past economic trends on the UK economy, the pamphlet revisits Labour's core values on the economy. It proposes a new approach to public sector deficits, to industrial intervention, and to financial reform. Labour needs to develop its thinking on all three if it is to have an economic manifesto for the next election which is attractive and credible, to both financial markets and voters.

1. LABOUR'S CREDIBILITY GAP

Credibility on economic policy is the holy grail of politics. If it can be obtained, the way ahead for a wide range of policies appears much clearer. Without economic credibility, it becomes almost impossible to convince the public of any other aspect of your policy agenda. All the policy ideas in the world are as worth nothing if Labour fails to learn this lesson afresh.

It still seems amazing that Labour lost its economic credibility. The 2010 General Election was lost in large part because Labour's message on the economy was confused and it had tarnished its reputation for sound economic management. It continues to be an effort for many on the Left to accept this point. If Labour had simply been outspun on economic policy despite getting everything right, that would have been bad enough. But Labour did not get everything right. It undermined its own reputation going into the financial crisis and even though it did the right things during the crisis its reputation for economic competence diminished further.

This must seem very unfair to those who were ministers during the financial crisis. They spent hours during crucial weekends banging bankers' heads together and engineering a bail out of the banking sector so large it made former nationalisations look quite inconsequential. They had to do so, because our economy was on the brink of collapse. When the inevitable recession struck, the Labour Government took action to promote job creation, bring forward investment spending, and support struggling companies. It also authorised a round of quantitative easing, permitting the Bank of England to print money to sustain the banking system and expand nominal demand. The Conservative Party opposed each step, alternating between calling for cuts in government spending and playing catch-up with developing economic policy. Yet despite this, Labour struggled to explain its case going into the 2010 election, which it lost badly with 29 per cent of the vote.

There are various ways in which Labour's economic credibility has been damaged. Labour undermined its own reputation for prudence before the financial crisis by letting borrowing rise without a clear explanation for how it would be reduced or how spending would always be relevant to voters' priorities. While those borrowing levels now appear low, what was undermined was the faith that taxpayers and investors could have that Labour could take the necessary steps. Labour also bought into the neo-liberal consensus on how financial markets should be regulated, ignoring (along with many) the lessons of past disasters. There is little evidence of convincing attempts to challenge that consensus.[1] In practice there was no dividing line here with the Conservatives. In the midst of the crisis, Labour made the right decisions, but had to do so while adjusting its politics and this made it difficult to explain to voters. Finally, Labour sometimes forgot to stand its economic policy firmly on the foundations of its political values.

Building economic credibility

Labour spent years in opposition building up its reputation for soundness on economic matters. This reputation was maintained in government but as the years progressed policy became captured by a free market consensus. Following conventional wisdom is not the same thing as establishing sustainable credibility, as the Conservatives will probably discover before too long. To restore economic credibility, Labour has to rediscover its earlier spirit and combine sensible economics with progressive politics once more.

Labour understood the need for economic credibility in the 1990s and worked hard to present a rigorous and thought-through economic platform. At the same time it sought to improve its relationship with the City – the so-called 'prawn cocktail offensive'. It was helped by the blow to public trust in the Conservatives' economic management following sterling's brutal ejection from the European Exchange Rate Mechanism (ERM) in 1992 and the recession during which it took place. The economic and cross-party consensus in 1990 was that sterling should join the ERM. The Conservatives struggled to recover from our exit despite economic policy-making becoming more transparent afterwards. By the following year, the Conservative poll lead on economic management had been lost; apart from a brief bounce in the run up to the 1997 election, it was not until the middle of the financial crisis that it was regained.[2] It took years to wipe away voters' memories of 1992.

Labour still had work to do. It developed a reputation for fiscal prudence, the then Shadow Chancellor, Gordon Brown, announced there would be clear fiscal rules and he put firm restrictions on the spending promises of his colleagues, ultimately with a commitment to match Conservative spending plans for two years after 1997.

In government, Labour raised a windfall tax on utilities to pay for the New Deal project to tackle youth unemployment and auctioned mobile phone wireless frequencies. These factors, together with a recovering economy, helped Labour achieve key aims while bringing down government debt and moving the public finances to an annual surplus. Moreover, Labour handed implementation of monetary policy to an independent Bank of England.

Labour's fiscal rules helped discipline the Government and encourage the electorate and markets to be confident that public finances would be kept under control. The rules were:

- The current account would be balanced over the economic cycle, with longer term borrowing only for investment.
- Net debt would not exceed 40 per cent of GDP.

The rules were instrumental in helping reinforce Labour's reputation for economic prudence. Compliance was monitored by investors as a guide to the extent to which the Government was maintaining sound public finances. The rules themselves were somewhat arbitrary. They relied upon an accurate estimate of the economic cycle at any given time. The net debt/GDP limit of 40 per cent was well below the European Maastricht limit of 60 per cent and could as easily have been, say, 45 per cent or 50 per cent. Together with an independent Bank of England – one of the boldest moves Labour made on economic policy – the intention was to create the conditions for macro economic stability. This would be the end of 'boom and bust' under which it was held that arbitrary political decisions gave rise to more volatile economic conditions. Labour has appeared to follow a form of neoclassical synthesis which holds that Keynes' General Theory applies to the special case of sharp downturns with conventional economic models applying otherwise. This ruled out the practice of past Governments to manipulate demand which led to boom-bust policies (but it did not challenge prevailing economic consensus). The stable policy framework would enable businesses to be more confident in the future, and therefore more likely to invest.

Success, erosion of credibility, and then the crisis

Labour presided over 44 quarters of positive growth from 1997 to 2007. This coincided with the latter half of the period christened the 'Great Moderation' (which began somewhere around the late 1980s). During this period, leading Western economies appeared to be stable with low but continuous growth and low inflation. The development of emerging economies such as China enabled goods to be produced at lower cost. As the emerging economies exported, they funded Western economy public sector deficits by, for example, buying US Treasury bonds in order to keep interest rates low. The UK benefited from the low inflation environment. The apparent stability encouraged private borrowing

As the bubble grew, the rise and celebration of the super rich coincided with stagnation in living standards for many.

and as the financial sector expanded, so its tax revenues were recycled to fund policy objectives including redistribution. This was a model in which many across the political spectrum put their faith; the Conservatives agreed with Labour's spending plans for example.

There was much that was creditable about Labour's economic record and which would have been the envy of Governments past (that is still the case after the crisis, given the action on unemployment). It was not a given that Britain would itself enjoy the Great Moderation's years of low inflation and steady growth. Government policy supporting it was essential: the independent Bank of England acted as a guarantor of low inflation; unemployment fell to a low of 1.4 million; fiscal discipline ensured the money could be found to build and equip new schools and hospitals and properly fund our public services; and a minimum wage and improved rights for workers improved the lives of many. Furthermore, by keeping out of the euro we ensured the UK economy maintained maximum flexibility to deal with a downturn. Somehow, though, as the financial bubble grew, the rise and celebration of the super rich coincided with stagnation in living standards for many. The contrast was sharp before the crisis struck. The abolition of the 10p income tax rate further confused people about our priorities. While Labour's opinion poll lead on the economy remained, the public had little optimism about the economy.[3]

A new narrative was growing. Labour had built its economic reputation over many years through fiscal prudence, limits on personal tax rates, and by gaining credibility with economic experts. However, in later years a perception grew that most people were ignored when economic policy was made. What's more, there was little in the way of a clear message other than that Labour was on the side of hard-working families (it was hardly the opposite) and the earlier optimism about a stakeholder economy relevant to people on all income levels was lost. The burden of taxation seemed to be getting higher while inflation was moving well ahead of earnings and this squeezed the middle. Companies turfed people off final benefit pension schemes, increasing their risks in later life, and somehow this was just accepted as inevitable. The increases in public spending were less appreciated than they had been because they did not appear to match the gains and there was little outward sign that the public sector was determined to become more efficient and cost effective.

The message on public spending that Labour was for investment but the Conservatives were for spending cuts worked well
with the public who remembered the years of underinvestment
in public services under Thatcher and Major. People supported
Labour on this because they could see that such investment
could produce decent returns – in the form of shorter waiting
times for operations, say, or improving state schools – and they
were right. This investment-versus-cuts argument lost power
when people began to doubt the returns they would get from
'investing' their income via taxation. Labour had refuted its reputation for tax and spend by keeping tax rates down. It now left
itself open to the charge again, not due to economic irresponsibility but because spending decisions in government seemed
less accountable. This was part reality and part perception but
the political impact was real. Labour entered the financial crisis
politically much weaker on the economy than it should have
been and with an open goal for Conservative propaganda about
Labour taxing and spending.

For many years, Labour's compliance with the fiscal rules
was held as an indication of its economic soundness. Initially,
meeting them appeared straightforward. As this changed, compliance with the first rule (balance across a cycle and borrow
only to invest) was difficult to demonstrate given ambiguity
about when the Treasury expected the cycles to end. The structural deficit, borrowing that would stay throughout the cycle,
ahead of the recession was at 3.3 per cent of national income –
one of the largest in the OECD.[4] Prudence is not about just meeting fiscal rules; it is about making absolutely sure one does so.[5]
Gradually Labour's reputation in the City for prudence was
undermined.

When the financial crisis struck in 2007, the UK Government
net debt/GDP ratio was below 40 per cent, at 36.5 per cent.[6] At
this level it was well below many other rich countries but

towards the limit of the golden rule. Such was the scale of the crisis and recession that this starting level didn't really seem to matter at first given that it was dwarfed by the expanding deficit. We know that after the crisis Labour ministers recognised there was a credibility issue because they introduced the Financial Stability Act, which committed the Government to halving the deficit over four years. The UK did not enter the crisis with public finances 'out of control' but with credibility in them eroded.

Through prompt action, Labour, saved the UK economy from depression. Despite gloomy predictions that unemployment would rise to over 4 million, the increase was much less than expected (though the outlook has deteriorated over the past year). The Chancellor, Alistair Darling, presented budget statements which indicated how the deficit would be brought under control.

Yet despite this, Labour struggled to explain its case going into the 2010 election. No party won that election and the Conservatives did not convince the public to put them into government. However, Labour had lost the economic case with the electorate. Labour had had to change direction on economic policy in order to do the right thing during the crisis and in some way the crisis appeared in some people's minds to epitomise their discomfort with the Party. Doubts that had grown before the crisis were reinforced by the high levels of borrowing required to fight it. The financial crisis was Labour's 1992 moment.

Financial credibility

The financial crisis may have been one of Gordon Brown's finest hours[7] but he and Alistair Darling have received little credit for this (indeed, many people today would probably scoff at the idea). Brown played to his strengths, co-ordinating and leading international action to rescue the banking system and lead a way out of global recession. The UK took bold action after the fall of Lehman Brothers in September 2008 by taking stakes in UK banks in addition to measures designed to increase liquidity in the monetary system. The circumstances required crisis management and some bold decisions. In the UK, these were taken, and they were followed in various ways by similar efforts around the world.

The *political* problem is that the decisions to bail out the banks were bold at the time because they went so much against the grain of Labour's previous policy. The Government had judged that 'light touch' financial regulation was positive for the UK's standing in the world and the growth of its financial sector. The Conservative Party was more fervent in this belief. The increasing sophistication of financial markets had persuaded policymakers and regulators around the world that risk was better managed. This was despite JK Galbraith's maxim that all financial innovation comes down to different ways to increase debt.[9]

Perhaps most pervasive was the self-assurance in the banking sector that it understood how the world worked and how to make a great deal of money from it. The financial sector was not only large, it exerted political power too. The long period of relative financial stability had led to complacency about the risks that were being taken. New and complicated financial products were invented and declared to be low risk. Little attention was paid to systemic risk, and regulation was based on how the world was meant to work, not how it worked in practice. Running through these times of increasing risk and complacency was a strong consensus, akin to the pro-ERM consensus in 1990, amongst regulators, economists, and policy-makers that freer financial markets were more efficient and therefore more desirable. Labour agreed.

The belief that freer markets were better markets combined with the political reluctance of a left-of-centre Government to be associated with nationalisation. The travails of Northern Rock illustrate the point. The bank believed it had a highly profitable business model but ignored the risks. It suffered as confidence fell and depositors withdrew funds. The Bank of England was concerned with moral hazard – that intervention might encourage other banks to take risks. The Labour Government was later concerned to do everything possible to avoid the obvious course of action: nationalising Northern Rock. Ultimately, the right thing was done but not out of conviction. The conviction came later.

These factors also help explain the lack of bold action over the following year, between the fall of Northern Rock and the bailouts of Royal Bank of Scotland, Lloyds TSB, and HBOS in October 2008. This was despite markets being distinctly unhealthy throughout that period. In the United States, the collapse of Lehman Brothers could have been avoided if the US administration had not been so wedded to an extreme free market philosophy, as Anatole Kaletsky emphasises. The Labour Government deserves credit for leading the way by recapitalising banks, but it still took three weeks after the Lehmans collapse for that to happen. There was no manual for a crisis on such a scale but the direct intervention, while necessary, required a major shift in Labour's economic narrative. (It was not alone in this, after all, a Republican President had to do the same).

What were the criteria that made intervention so necessary? Surely not such an abyss of imminent disaster as the one Darling and colleagues were staring down during that crucial October weekend? While the intervention saved the financial system from collapse, we still do not know if it took the best form. Arguably, it should have required more of banks. The shift in Labour's thinking about the financial sector, and economic policy in general, is continuing today.

Labour's economic plans

The financial crisis led to a sharp drop in economic confidence and activity across the economy. Tax revenues fell and variable government spending rose as people lost their jobs or worked part time. In addition, the Government implemented some stimulus measures, such as cutting VAT. The combined result was that government borrowing rose steeply, with the annual deficit at one point predicted to peak at around 80 per cent of GDP, later revised down to 75 per cent (and to 74 per cent by the OBR before Osborne's first budget). The Darling plan, outlined in his 2010 Budget, sought to cut public borrowing sharply. The deficit would be halved within four years. To do this, Darling proposed collecting an extra £24bn of tax and cutting spending by £47bn (after some spending was protected, spending in other areas would have to fall by £50.8bn of which £44.1bn was not specified).[10] He described these spending cuts as more severe than those imposed under Margaret Thatcher in the early 1980s. Stimulus measures would begin to be unwound from April 2010.

The Tory-Liberal Dem austerity ideology will face severe strain if economies experience years of little or no growth.

It is highly likely, however, that had Labour won the 2010 election, Darling would have had to present an emergency budget statement ahead of the autumn spending review. He was treading a fine line between avoiding damaging the recovery and assuaging the holders and buyers of UK government debt. He largely succeeded – for which he deserves more credit – but Labour's credibility in markets had been damaged. In addition, markets and the economic establishment were getting in a panic about the Greek debt crisis. To prevent the cost of UK government debt rising in a market panic, Darling would have had to spell out in more detail the spending cuts he planned, and revised down his growth forecasts to more prudent figures.[11] Investors wanted to see evidence that the UK Government would follow through with cuts to actual spending programmes. We can see this was the case because it was not until the coalition's October spending review that Standard & Poor took the UK's AAA rating off 'negative outlook', despite Osborne's 'emergency' June budget. The coalition's error was to increase the – already severe – spending cuts from Labour's plans.

Given that the Darling plan has been advocated by Labour in opposition, we should note that it relied upon economic growth picking up considerably more than it has done to date. Darling's forecasts of growth of 3.25 per cent in 2011 and 3.5 per cent in 2012, would have been revised lower. The OBR forecasts before Osborne's first budget last year predicted growth of 2.6 per cent in 2011 and 2.8 per cent in 2012 (since revised lower, to 1.7 per cent and 2.5 per cent respectively).[12] In the fiscal year 2010/11, the coalition Government largely followed Labour's Budget plans. The second and third quarters of 2010 saw encouraging growth but the economy has since been flat, due to poor winter weather and a lacklustre subsequent bounce. Endless talk of spending cuts probably dented a fragile recovery. Nevertheless, it would still have snowed under a Labour Government in December 2010, when GDP declined.

If another recession were to occur – a so-called 'double dip' – this could damage the coalition. A slowdown can be accommodated in the short term under its fiscal targets because they allow for higher spending on welfare and unemployment payments and because if inflation fell the Bank of England could print more money. But in a double dip or extended period of limited growth, the coalition's economic gamble would be discredited and it would have to abandon its whole fiscal stance if it wanted to stimulate investment or consumer spending. Similarly, the Tory-Liberal Democrat austerity ideology will face severe strain if economies experience years of little or no growth, made worse by premature spending cuts. But politics is about choices and Labour would itself need to provide a credible alternative that was not simply its own version of a 'Plan B' for the economy, but a longer term idea of what sort of economy we need. As things stand, Labour may even find itself blamed if the coalition capitulates and increases borrowing.

Restoring economic credibility

Labour has to restore its economic credibility. It can win as many battles as it likes elsewhere but the prime focus must be on economic policy. On the one hand, the party will not restore its credibility on the economy by wearing sackcloth and ashes when talking about its record, as much as the Conservatives would like us to; playing down what we got right in government would be particularly masochistic, especially given the bold action Labour took during and after the financial crisis.

However, the opposite mistake – to underplay what Labour got wrong – would be equally misguided. That does not mean we own up to errors the Conservatives claim we made. The finances were not out of control before the financial crisis.[13] The new Government did not find that Britain was bankrupt. Nevertheless, the Conservative re-writing of history has become entrenched.

What we must do is acknowledge, as Shadow Chancellor Ed Balls began to do in his 2011 Budget response, that we, along with others, followed the prevailing economic consensus too far. Doing otherwise would have encountered great resistance from a powerful banking lobby but we should have made the attempt. Liam Byrne, leading Labour's policy review, has highlighted the pressures on the 'squeezed middle' pre-dated the financial crisis.[14] These statements show Labour is keen to learn the lessons of its defeat.

To restore economic credibility, Labour needs to be clear that its credibility problem began before the crisis. Amidst all the good things it did, people sensed they were not sharing the experience of the good times. The crisis forced Labour to reset policy. That the Tories committed to match our previous plans matters little now to voters. People are concerned about the state of the economy, as consumer confidence and opinion polling data suggest. They are also concerned about the speed and extent of deficit reduction and the outlook for their financial situation. However, Labour is still blamed for the deficit.[15]

Labour cannot restore economic credibility simply by finding the right words to say about the past and this must be more than a debate about the timing of spending cuts. We need an economic vision which is both progressive and rooted in reality. We cannot repeat previous totemic acts, such as changing Clause IV, that changed people's perception of Labour.

The task ahead for Eds Miliband and Balls is in some ways much harder. Labour must start with the following:

- **Reaffirm core values that are essential for a progressive economic policy**
  There is a good debate starting around this at the moment but it needs to lead to policy and an account of the robust decisions Labour would take. How can we ensure people have a stake in their economy?

- **Promote a more equal society through all aspects of economic policy**
  This is about remembering who economic policy is for. We should not be relaxed at people getting filthy rich if that happens in a way which works against the common good and risks a new crisis. We should promote a society in which the *contribution* to growth is more widely shared and where the proceeds are justly shared. Every UK citizen should have an active stake in their economy, with an active Government promoting opportunity, investing in its people, and encouraging aspiration.

- **Be clear what we think about budget deficits and what we will do about them**
  The coalition Government is taking a big risk with its deficit-cutting plans but it does so within a centre-right consensus that these plans are essential. Progressives need to be clear about when deficits are necessary and where extra spending would be directed. We must show how they would put the public finances in better shape. Saying either that we would cut, but not by quite as much, or that we will cut by some underdetermined amount some time in the future, is not sufficient.

  Furthermore, any strategy of paying homage to the Darling Plan has to be adapted for lower growth and new economic aims. Labour must welcome the Office for Budget Responsibility as a good thing and commit to retaining it. Labour must describe the circumstances when it will run a deficit and where any stimulus will be directed.

- **Labour should make a covenant with the people**
  It will maintain tight control over spending, especially relative to tax. It should work on an 'effective spending guarantee'. Shadow frontbenchers must show how they buy into this.

- **Demonstrate an understanding of economic realities, including the power of the bond markets**
  The Treasury got spooked last year when Greece came under pressure in the bond markets, fearing the UK might next be subject to falling investor sentiment. That played into Conservative smaller-state ideology. Nevertheless, international capital markets are important, like it or not. We cannot just ignore them and hope they go away.

- **Understand the needs of business… and finance**
  Labour's debates on work and prosperity policy need to be clearly informed about how business works and how finance is essential. Intervention has its place and we need new mechanisms and a new culture for it, but the Left must focus on encouraging more investment longer term.

- **Relearn to love a (reformed) City**
  Linked to the point above. The banks need to be reformed but the City is more than just the banks. The

financial sector represents at least 8 per cent of GDP. Labour should engage with it.

- **Focus on the concerns people will have in 2015, looking ahead to 2020 and beyond**
  We need to win battles now but we must not lose sight of this longer term goal or people will think we are more concerned about the past than their future.

Key charge	The Conservative position	The Labour position
Labour let the crisis, and then the deficit, happen. It promoted light regulation and did not question financial market power.	The Conservative approach at the time was to promote less regulation and, during the crisis, to argue for spending to be cut.	The roots of the financial crisis were in the US housing market. Global investment banks, including those based in the UK, became particularly exposed. Labour engineered a bail-out of the banking system.
Spending got out of control under Labour before the crisis.	Conservatives pledged to match Labour's spending commitments.	Labour's 2007 spending review was tougher than its predecessor.
Spending continued at high levels during the crisis.	The deficit was unnecessary and a sign of economic failure.	Spending levels were maintained and increased into the recession while tax revenues fell. To do otherwise would have risked another Great Depression.
The politics of the crisis were mishandled. Labour did not have a robust explanation of what it thought about high annual deficits and what it planned to do about them.	The Conservatives opposed each stage of action to tackle the crisis until the last moment. Had their approach been followed, we might still be in recession. However, as the recession came to a technical end, Conservatives played well on the growing unease with high debt levels.	The politics trailed the action. Labour became more interventionist and rejected its previous light tough regulatory approach to banks.

Table 1: Comparing Conservative and Labour positions

2. WHAT HAPPENED AND WHERE WE ARE NOW

The financial crisis caused confidence and activity to drop sharply across the UK economy. Output continues to remain below pre-crisis levels and real incomes have been hit. Inequality remains a central problem.

There are many fine accounts of the financial crisis but what interests us here is what it did to the UK economy and what form the recovery has taken.

The financial trigger

The financial crisis really occurred over a couple of years, from mid 2007. A prolonged period of economic stability and low interest rates provided the conditions for greater risk-taking in the financial sector. As investors chased yield, so new financial products were created to meet their demand. US mortgage debt in particular was repackaged and sold on in the form of financial securities. By diversifying and structuring the debt, banks believed they had managed the risks away and allowed their gearing levels (debt compared to equity) to rise to record levels.[16]

Low interest rates helped encourage a house price boom in the US and elsewhere, providing a steady stream of debt to be sold on. Central banks acted against consumer price inflation but not against asset price inflation. Regulatory changes designed to promote home ownership under both Clinton and Bush administrations provided a further stimulus. Helping people on low incomes to own their own homes was seen as a worthwhile aim, but it required more borrowing to be achieved. The pressures for such a policy in the US were acute, since the levels of inequality were high and politicians were confronted with a growing perception that few were able to live the American Dream. In this case however, rule changes permitted people to participate in the house price bubble with the consequence that they also participated in the crash. For many, what little assets they had turned into large unserviceable debts, and the systemic problems began.[17]

The US housing market began to turn in 2007 and for a while the financial sector carried on regardless despite crumbling foundations. In the UK, Northern Rock took more risks in the mortgage market. When a couple of hedge funds began to falter in the summer, investors took fright. The market for esoteric securities closed. The banking model, of borrowing short term to lend long term, had been taken to extremes. Northern Rock was a prime example. Investors demanded higher interest rates to lend to banks even over the short term and, in the case of Northern Rock, began to refuse to lend. Retail depositors took fright and tried to withdraw their savings. Northern Rock cracked.

Financial markets remained seized up over the following year, with banks having to pay high interest rates to borrow funds. This was because no one was quite sure what toxic debt banks had on their balance sheets. Central banks tried to help by cutting their interest rates and lending to the banking system. The US investment bank Bear Stearns faced trouble in 2008 and was bought by JP Morgan. By September 2008 the US had intervened to bail out government mortgage companies Fannie Mae and Freddie Mac. Then Lehman Brothers became the focus of market attention. A reluctance by the US Government to directly bail out banks in trouble ensured Lehmans was allowed to go bankrupt. However, so many banks (including those with high street banking arms) were exposed to securities which Lehmans traded that this free market approach made things worse. The US changed tack and rescued insurance firm AIG. Confidence in the banking system collapsed with, at one stage, even the viability of ordinary payments systems in doubt. In October the British Government changed the rules of the game and directly recapitalised Royal Bank of Scotland, Lloyds TSB, and HBOS.

The crisis of confidence would continue into 2009 (requiring further bank recapitalisation) and by now the banking crisis directly threatened the global economy. Banks cut lending as they sought to rebuild balance sheets. At the same time, business confidence dropped. Thus began the deepest UK recession since the 1930s. Concerned at the state of the banking sector and the drop in the money supply, in early 2009 the Government authorised the Bank of England to begin Quantitative Easing (QE) – the electronic equivalent of printing money. By increasing the money supply in this way, the authorities aimed to boost nominal GDP (inflation plus real growth). The Bank injected £200bn. That money supply growth has remained low or non existent indicates how necessary was this policy.

The UK economy responds

The fall in income at the end of 2008 and beginning of 2009 was dramatic. In six months, GDP fell 6.4 per cent. This was deeper than the 1930s recession and the low came earlier but the economy initially recovered at the same rate as the 1980s recovery. Figure 1, below, compares this recession with the past two, taking the starting points as the previous GDP high. The data show that GDP fell in the Q4 2010 and rose in Q1 2011, implying a flat six month period. The preliminary estimate for growth in Q2 2011 showed the economy barely growing at all. The rate of recovery so far remains comparable however. Decisions made now, on spending and on eurozone sovereign debt, have the potential to knock us off course.

These figures are subject to later revisions and indeed some of the forward-looking economic data point to a more vibrant economy. Note that if we follow the Bank of England and take the beginning of the 1980s recession as beginning a couple of quarters later (quarter 2 in Figure 1), the recent recession will look comparably worse. The observations about the rate of recoveries do not change however.

All the major economies suffered a sharp slowdown after the Lehman Brothers collapse (some had been slowing beforehand). Yet while economies such as Germany and France have more or less recovered their output levels and the US is close, the UK, along with Spain, has not.

If we break down UK economic performance by output, it can be seen that production fell significantly in the recession, with the service sector (which includes government spending) holding up relatively well (see Figure 2).

The Office for Budget Responsibility (OBR) projections contain a powerful boost to private investment, of around nine per cent a year from 2010 to 2015. We do not in fact know when companies will boost investment significantly beyond rebuilding their inventories after the recession, the next leg of the recovery. The OBR also forecasts an increase

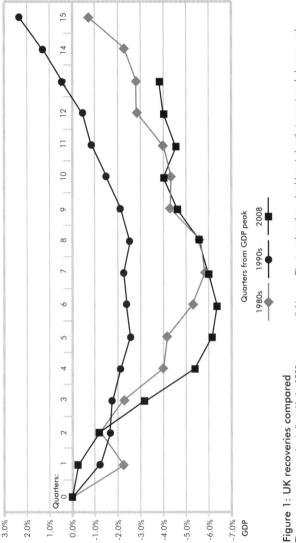

Figure 1: UK recoveries compared
The economy was recovering in line with the 1980s recovery until this year. Charts such as these should remind us that recessions do happen and economies do recover. The risk however is that bad policy decisions can stifle a recovery and lead to years of low or no growth, with negative consequences for jobs. *Source: Office for National Statistics dataset.*

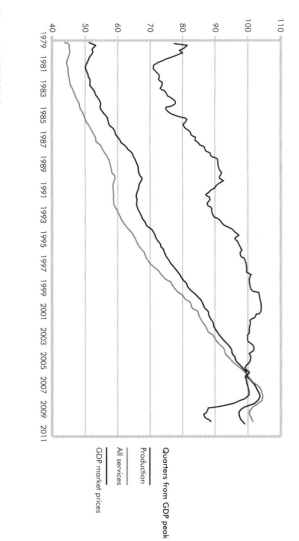

Figure 2: UK GDP by category
Not surprisingly, production was hit hard in the recession. Private sector investment fell substantially as confidence dropped across most sectors in the economy. Getting businesses to invest again at healthy levels is the major challenge. *Source: Office for National Statistics dataset.*

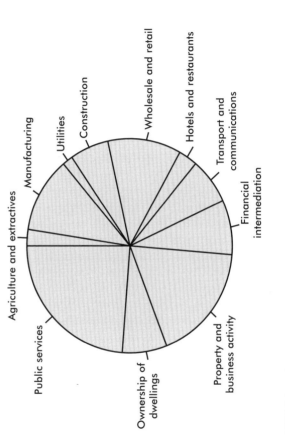

Figure 3: UK GDP 2010 by category
The UK is primarily a service economy, with 75 per cent of output from service sectors of some kind. Manufacturing forms around 11 per cent and the financial sector represents 8 per cent of output. *Source: Office for National Statistics dataset.*

in net exports. The value of the pound on the foreign exchanges fell by 30 per cent in the crisis and it remains 25 per cent below pre crisis levels. Exports, of which around half are from manufacturing, have yet to respond though adjustments can take time and much depends on growth in world markets. While firms can use the cheaper pound to cut prices and gain market share, they may initially choose to raise their export prices and take higher profits. If they have been keeping workers on during the downturn this will have been an attractive option as they sought to rebuild profit margins.

Unemployment rose, but the most pessimistic predictions did not come about. Overall, unemployment peaked (to date) at 2.5 million, or 8 per cent. This compares with a high of around 3.3 million (12 per cent) in the 1980s recession. The impact is felt particularly by young people, with youth unemployment at 20 per cent or higher. There is also a large number of people in part time employment who want full time jobs. The sudden drop in economic activity across all sectors may have encouraged firms to hold onto labour in expectation of recovery. They took a short-term hit to profit margins to do so. The Labour Government's public support for the economy also played its part.

Meanwhile, most people with debt have experienced the benefits of low interest rates. The Bank of England cut its rate to 0.5 per cent in 2008 and kept it at this level. Households with a mortgage will have benefited but the gap between the Bank's rate and market rates for mortgages is higher than before the financial crisis. Savers have suffered, with declines in the real value of their wealth and income. The Bank has combined low interest rates with Quantitative Easing to pump money (£200bn) into the economy and the summer of 2011 saw speculation by some that it might decide to initiate another round of QE.

Inflation has stubbornly persisted at a level above the Bank's 2 per cent target. In large part this is due to rises in food and energy prices. These external factors have pushed up the price index. Average wage increases have remained low, at just over 2 per cent. The squeeze on real incomes has therefore been very apparent and the income available for discretionary spending (in other words, not on bills and taxes) is likely to fall for the average household in 2011 unless consumers borrow more and save less. The Bank Governor, Mervyn King, noted that in 2011 on a net basis consumers would see incomes fall over six years for the first time since the 1920s. If wages begin to increase in line with the inflation level we might fear that inflation was becoming a domestic problem. So far, it has largely been due to pressures in the global economy, particularly in growing emerging markets. External price shocks eventually drop out of the inflation figures but persistent inflation in food and energy markets could pose a serious problem. Living standards would continue to fall.[19]

The financial crisis began with consumer borrowing at high levels. The savings ratio reached a low of -0.9 per cent in 2008. The ratio rose to 7.5 per cent in the recession in 2009 before falling back to 4.6 per cent at the beginning of 2011. Data released by the OBR shows its growth forecasts depend on an increase in household borrowing but, boldly perhaps, not on an increase in mortgages. The OBR assumes people will want to maintain their standard of living and, in the face of falling real incomes, will borrow to do so. This seems a depressing assumption because it implies the way to recovery includes some repeat of our past behaviour.[20]

Inequality, at least as measured by the Gini co-efficient, has risen since it was measured in the 1960s, peaking in 2007. The Reagan-Thatcher revolution saw inequality increase in Britain. It fell after the 1990s recession, rose in Labour's first term, declined in the second, and rose to its highest level since the 1960s just before this recession. However, the Institute for Fiscal Studies notes that inequality actually *declined* for the middle 60 per cent of the income distribution during Labour's time in office. In addition, relative poverty declined during Labour's period in office for a sustained period until the third term, before the slowdown. A small proportion of the population at the top of the income distribution saw incomes rise far ahead of the rest.[21] This snapshot looks only at income levels; it does not highlight the pressures people on low and middle incomes have faced with higher spending required on food and fuel bills.[22] The IFS notes that while median household incomes rose slightly between 2007-8 and 2009-10 due to welfare payments and state support, in 2010-11 "earnings, state benefits and tax credits all fell in real terms" and it estimates median net household income fell 3.5 per cent, back to the 2003-4 level and the biggest single-year drop since 1981. It believes the decline in living standards will continue to 2013-14.[23]

Under Labour, some progress was made against strong global headwinds. Nevertheless, inequality remains one of the central problems of our time both in terms of social justice, and by distorting our market economy and often encouraging borrowing. The problem may be compounded by an ageing population, which will increase the claim on resources.

Coalition economic policy is based on the assumption, or hope, that reducing government spending before recovery is underway will lead to a miraculous private sector expansion. The gamble is that acting so tough on the deficit will boost economic confidence rather than undermine it as spending cuts hit overall demand; so far there is little evidence the gamble is paying off. This year will be important as spending cuts begin to bite. Some sort of further recovery is highly likely and only natural given the depth of the recession but it may be limited because this recovery has occurred with credit conditions still tight rather than easing as in past upturns and government spending is being cut so harshly so soon. Although households remain relatively indebted, the corporate sector balance sheet seems strong so there is scope for an increase in private sector investment if businesses feel confident in the future.

The options available to Chancellors are limited in the short term. Changes to tax and spending take time to implement and sometimes have unexpected consequences. Longer term, Chancellors can influence the direction the economy takes, via fundamental reforms and by affecting business confidence via their contribution to minimising uncertainty. The current incumbent holds to a particular economic worldview and political ideology which means he is willing to take the risk that growth might not be sufficient for him to meet his harsh fiscal plans, while frontloading spending cuts with harsh implications for many. His rhetoric and action on austerity have helped keep the growth rate down.

The UK economy is still experiencing a readjustment from the pre-crisis days. Global sovereign debt concerns have dented business confidence and even manufacturing growth appears to have stalled. The coalition Government has given us one clear model which risks the recovery both because government spending is being cut back harshly and quickly, and because it risks denting confidence which businesses and consumers need if they are to be more economically active. It also ignores the lack of demand in the global economy and the risks to growth if every country does the same thing. As Ed Miliband has remarked, "collective austerity, advocated by our government, is too simplistic for the complex challenges the world faces."[24] A Labour alternative needs to be not only technically robust but consistent with its values and its vision for society.

3. CAN WE HAVE A 'GOOD ECONOMY'?

The Left must engage with economic policy if debates about the Good Society are to get anywhere. Our values are are consistent with a society in which virtue matters in markets, inequality is reduced, and economic power is dispersed.

The UK economy remains characterised by inequality with signs that any rebalancing that takes place may be focused on further declines in real incomes for most people. Labour now has to engage in deep thinking about the kind of economy we should have in future. Our values will be key.

One thing is for sure. We cannot simply hope that the coalition sorts out the deficit problem and, running out of energy, gives way to a Labour Government that can dust off the 1997 playbook, maintaining neo-liberal economic credibility while redistributing to the poorest. If we fight elections on that basis, we may have to wait some time for government. We need answers to the questions facing people today, not in the last century. Our values remain relevant; we need to show that we know how to apply them.

The Reagan-Thatcher economic revolution saw market values reasserted with neo-liberal economic theory dictating to politics as people became disillusioned, with good reason, with the corporatist big state approach of the 1970s.[25] It is ironic that today the 'big state' is seen as part of the problem given that the last decade has seen nothing like the grim stagflation of the 1970s. As the private sector became more involved in the provision of public services, so a new symbiotic relationship between business and state was formed. At the same time, the increasing power of the financial sector and financial market deregulation fed off each other. Political power was eroded, not simply through the size of the financial sector but through the shift in worldview and values which took place. While regulators were seduced by financial models which appeared to diversify away risk, politicians found their thinking constrained. It was difficult to think of concepts such as choice in public services outside of a consumerist market-led framework. By starting from a worldview that excluded fuzzy ideas such as the common good, it was impossible to lever them in later on. To be fair to the politicians, this transformation of values occurred throughout society. It prevails today, despite the financial crisis.

At this point we need to reaffirm, if somewhat wearily, that markets are not bad. They can be inappropriately applied and that is where the problems can start. Indeed, while the worlds of business and government can be very different (as most businesspeople entering politics discover, much to their chagrin), there is much to be said for the levels of rigour, attention to detail, and competitive discipline that can be found in the best businesses and financial companies. Very few in politics understand business and finance, and it shows (particularly in their adulation of high profile business leaders). But when we allow markets to determine our values, rather than exercising our values through markets, we become complicit in weakening our society.

In case this seems all rather esoteric, we should recall the impact on people outlined in the previous chapter. The neo-liberal triumph was built in part on the debt of many households and left us ill-prepared for the changes in the global economy as emerging economies grew rapidly.

In the halcyon days of Edwardian liberalism, Labour emerged as the answer to the questions posed by many: amidst such prosperity how could they stop being so poor and so powerless? The party which stood clearly for equality offered an attractive alternative to spent ideologies on offer elsewhere. When combined with ability and experience in 1945, Labour's relevance was overwhelming. Labour exists, not merely to mitigate the excesses of neo-liberal economics but to reform the economy so that it works for the many and not the few. That is what the country expects us to do; indeed, it is our duty.

Labour today does not lack experience. And with its values and heritage it is the only party equipped to provide the answers to the fundamental questions people have about the economy. The public looks to Labour to challenge conservative ideology from that foundation, while remaining rooted in the real world and focused on the common good.[26] If people want conservatism they will vote for the party that bears the name. That they did not vote for a Conservative Government in 2010 implies that people were not converted but were wary of Labour's economic credibility and lack of a clear progressive message.

The coalition has gone back to the 1980s, buying into a neo-liberal economic worldview. This is in contrast with some of the Big Society debates, in which this worldview is challenged (that is, by those not simply using Big Society rhetoric as a smokescreen for cuts). However, it is not clear what fundamental changes a Big Society approach would make to the economy.

Much of the political debate on the Left since the election has focused on the Good Society concept. The idea has been developed in response to the Big Society but drawing on thinking that goes back many years. It is rooted in a Left tradition that pre-dates post war big state politics, but it is also open to the charge that it has little to say on the economy. Good Society thinking tends to stress:

- strengthening democracy at all levels of society;
- reaffirming politics over economic interests;
- a new role for the state, more transparent and working in partnership with other parts of society;
- a more equal society, in terms of risk, wealth, and power; and
- a focus on the common good, particularly in the provision of public services.[27]

However, to talk about a 'good' society implies a sense of morality and a set of values. These must be applied to the economic questions of our times. It also raises a more general question: what does a good market economy look like?

The financial crisis was not simply a stock market bubble that was bursting. It was an existential crisis that threatened the faith many had in the future.[28] As the consequences spread to the wider economy, so did the feeling of powerless unease. This experience points to the need for economic policy to be rooted in some fundamental values. Reflections on morality should not be alien to progressives. They can be linked to the current debate about the Good Society and the sort of economy we want to have.

After the immediate crisis was over and amid a deep recession, attention turned to the ethical basis on which market behaviour was based. Prime Minister Gordon Brown, speaking at an event in St Paul's Cathedral before the London G20 summit in April 2009, addressed this theme. Brown argued that "Our financial system must be founded on the very same values that are at the heart of our family lives, neighbourhoods, and communities." He believed that a global ethic was possible because there exists "a single powerful moral sense demanding responsibility from all and fairness to all." A few months later, at a TUC conference, Rowan Williams, the Archbishop of Canterbury, continued the theme. He argued we should promote three components of a "three dimensional humanity": family, imagination, and mutual sympathy. Economic life should be guided by the virtues of "courage, intelligent and generous foresight, self-critical awareness and concern for balanced universal welfare," together with Christian virtues of faith, hope, and love. Underpinning much of the thinking on values was a desire to restore the basis of trust in markets.

In retrospect, Williams' TUC speech in November 2009 occurred just at the closing of a window of opportunity for ethical change which had been open for the previous twelve months. When apparent political and economic certainties

In our search for new inspiration we should of course be wary of harking back to a Golden Age that never existed.

crumbled, attention turned towards morality and trust. Many believed market behaviour had become amoral. Within the banking sector even there was a search for values.[29] However, while there was much agreement about what values were required, there was little said about how they could be made evident. Yet this general sense that individuals and companies should behave well remains. When they do otherwise somehow the very fabric of our society is torn. The recent public questioning of media ethics also illustrates this point.

As the banking sector returned to business as usual, helped by extensive government intervention, we heard less about values and more about the virtue of making a great deal of money.

We can encourage companies and others to act in a more ethical manner but unless the state defines what this should mean in practice, and ensures the appropriate incentives are in place, change cannot be guaranteed. Unfortunately, politicians' calls for moral markets were stymied by the MPs allowances scandal, an inability to think beyond the neoliberal consensus, and a reluctance to attempt any kind of structural reform of the economy. However, the sovereign debt crisis is challenging those old orthodoxies which have reasserted themselves and a new window of opportunity to reframe the debate on economics and finance may be opening.

The ethical socialists of the first half of the last century have much to offer us in terms of what they said about the value of human beings and the quality of life (the policy conclusions we draw today will be very different). These were important parts of their commitment to fight poverty. More recently, advocates of Blue Labour appear to draw inspiration from this pre-1945 era, though really they need to look at how Labour got a grip on policy development under Hugh Dalton after the fall of the Labour Government in 1931.[30] In our search for new inspiration we should of course be wary of harking back to a Golden Age that never existed (this is also a trap for Big Society advocates). However, the histories of garden cities and craft socialism do retain their attractions, for behind them is the notion that price should not drive everything we do. Quite where the onward tide of market forces should beach is not always easy to determine, but there are limits. We need to think beyond the debates about what private sector role should be played in health or education, important though those are. Are the incentives in society structured to act against the preservation of what we regard as important?

The Christian Socialist thinker RH Tawney wrote in 1920 about his concerns that he was living in an 'acquisitive society'.[31]

Tawney believed that people lived fulfilled lives when they were contributing in some way to the common good. A society based on consumerism was in some way unfulfilled. Tawney could not have imagined the world we live in today and certainly not one where credit has been so easily available. Of course many of the things we buy help us live happy and contented lives. Still, Tawney made an important point. The financial crisis exposed an extreme example of what happens when people ignore the common good. It also exposed how powerless most people are. Political power seems limited today against the business as usual pleas of the banking sector. How much more powerless do individual people feel in towns and cities up and down the country? Tawney developed a concept of freedom, in which economic and social freedom matter as well as civic freedom.[32] This resonates today in a society which is seeing people pay with their livelihoods and wellbeing for the mistakes of others. The ethical socialist concepts of equality and freedom can again be at the heart of a 21st Century Labour economic policy.

We can bring these observations on values, equality, and freedom and power, together with economic understanding to both critique the past few years' economic performance and to chart a course for a progressive economic policy for the future. The financial crisis was also a crisis of irresponsibility, which led to an unfair outcome and exposed the accumulation and distortion of economic power. A consequence has been a further erosion of trust and breakdown of relationships in our society. The economy of the future should be structured to prevent virtue being crowded out. It should be one in which all can participate and benefit regardless of their start in life. It should contain safeguards which prevent the accumulation of too much market power by a few.

This approach shows us that the Good Society concept needs much development. The focus should not be on political-versus-market power but on a properly functioning market economy. This is because such an economy requires values, equality, and dispersion of market power (more economic freedom). This is very different to full-blown unrestrained capitalism in which government is akin to a deity that has no intention of intervening. Good Society advocates should not hope for a new corporatism with a better balance of power between state and business (especially banks), but a more dynamic economy. Here might be the beginnings of a New Economic Fabianism, in which a proactive state is essential to ensure the economy works for everyone; the state neither sits back nor does it simply focus on redistribution and micro measures to correct market and social failure.

This approach would contrast with the current Blue Labour position. By playing down the role of the state as it does, Blue Labour finds itself with little to say about how government should act at the macro level to encourage growth and target spending. It thus concedes the main battleground for public support before it has started.

It would be a different approach from that taken by Labour in government. Economic policy cannot be a technocratic, ideology-free zone with government redistributing income and tweaking at the micro level. New Labour's starting assumptions prevented values being applied to economic policy. Government has to intervene to ensure markets work effectively, which means without concentration of power or distorted values.

It is an approach which avoids an obsession with the state, while not denying it a vital role. There is no getting away from the need for government to spend money to ensure the outcomes we want are delivered (though we must focus on priorities rather than total spending increases) but we often talk more about where we should spend money and from where we should take it, than about how we can make our market economy work for everyone.

This approach may also resonate across the political spectrum with those who believe that capitalism has failed to live up to their expectations. Such people believe that capitalism must work for all, and may even concede that the Left, when it abandons an apparent fixation with the state, may be right.[33]

There are very practical implications. Government needs to understand when market outcomes are seen as unfair (not merely undesirable) and act. Policies will need to enable people to have opportunities to acquire new skills and will therefore include high funding for education. Members of each generation should have opportunities to live a fulfilled life which do not depend on privilege and that requires some radicalism. This will be alongside a market with incentives to get on which makes effort worthwhile (including especially a better understanding of the impact of personal taxation and the marginal tax rates people face) and a robust Government willing to stand up to monopolies and the undue accumulation of economic power wherever it lies.

Labour needs to be clear about what it stands for on the economy before it tries to produce a detailed policy platform. This may be why there has been uncertainty about the direction of the various policy reviews since the election. We do not have to take a big leap from values to policies. When we do that there is no thread linking our programme for government with the reasons why we want to be in government. We will give speeches about progressive values but we will risk our policies appearing to be small in comparison.[34] Between values such as equality and social justice, and policies, we need to tell the story in broad terms about why our values are so attractive and how we will seek to implement them in this country. This story is the bridge between our values and our policies.

Practical considerations do matter. Labour will make little progress unless it expands its current thinking about what a Good Society should look like to include economic implications. If we are going to make any kind of difference we need to show how we can make the tough decisions required on the economy. For Labour, being tough should not mean buying into a neo-liberal worldview at the expense of the poor and nor should it mean pursuing some sort of ideological social engineering. Whether we are talking about the Good Society, or Blue Labour, or whatever fresh idea or catchphrase next emerges, we must speak with authenticity. Our policies must be consistent with our values and we must provide answers to the pressing questions of today (high deficits, decline in living standards, 8 per cent unemployment) and tomorrow (our aspirations in life, the challenges of globalism and climate change), which for many means worthwhile work and the opportunity to live a fulfilled life.

Labour suffers from a confused message on the deficit. Deficit reduction could be slower than the coalition plans if it is in the context of a clear and credible economic plan. However, high deficits have to be dealt with and Labour needs an 'effective spending guarantee'.

A very clear alternative to the coalition Government's economic programme is to argue that few if any spending cuts are needed at all. This is a line we have heard from some trade unions and others. Advocates of maintaining a relatively large deficit argue that the economist JM Keynes, were he alive today, would have agreed. The argument is that it is wrong to rein back spending when the economy is only starting to recover. Deficits should rise in a recession and growth should remove them over time.

This is a reasonable position to take as long as people are convinced we mean to control spending and reduce it when growth has picked up sufficiently. We also need to convince the bond markets. Many countries are finding that debt reduction plans and growth plans must go together and must be convincing. This is why economic credibility is so important. If a party's reputation has been undermined, the more work it has to do to convince both markets and taxpayers, even if it is right.

The deficit-delayers argue that the British economy faces the prospect of years of low economic and employment growth. This country has sustained deficits of 200 per cent of GDP in the past; these were brought down by growth. Labour's policies should focus on investment, led by government, to drive future growth, and the maintenance of government spending to ensure public sector workers do not become unemployed. The deficit will look after itself and markets will adjust, especially when austerity measures begin to stymie growth in our European neighbours. Harsh spending cuts will distort any recovery that does occur and store up further problems for the future.

This is an attractive proposition because there is a lot of truth in it. As the global economy plunged into recession in 2008, a Keynesian approach became popular once more and countries took action to stimulate their economies. In the UK, rising unemployment triggered the 'automatic stabilisers' (in other words, more public money spent on welfare payments), and spending was maintained while tax revenues fell. These were the main influences on public debt. Labour did more by cutting VAT, bringing forward some capital spending, providing cash incentives for new car purchases, and postponing payment of tax. These measures provided a fiscal stimulus. Labour went into the General Election with the extra stimulus largely being unwound but with a large annual deficit. It also committed to halve that deficit in four years.

Economies such as Ireland, Greece, and Portugal are facing much more severe cuts (because they started from a worse position) and European economies are reducing their deficits. Italy came under pressure in the summer of 2011 because it had a relatively high *net debt* position (around 120 per cent of GDP) even though it was running a primary budget surplus. Prompted by the European Central Bank, the Italian Government brought forward its austerity plans. Spanish Government bonds were also sold off. The UK Government plans sharp cuts to spending to an extent that has attracted worldwide attention. The United States, however, had delayed significant cuts to its borrowing levels and even boosted its fiscal stimulus. Over the summer of 2011, in a last-minute deal to raise the debt ceiling, US politicians agreed deficit reduction measures. France too, faced with market anxiety, felt compelled to emphasise plans to reduce its deficit. In his book, *Beyond the Crash*, Gordon Brown argues that world leaders should work for a global stimulus to avoid the next ten years being characterised by low growth. This seems unlikely to occur unless economic growth falters significantly and by then it could be too late.

Perhaps the best argument for maintaining the deficit and focusing on growth was articulated by Labour's Shadow Chancellor, Ed Balls, when he was running for the leadership of the Labour Party.[35] He argued that the UK economy had faced higher deficits in the past due to wars. The financial crisis was another "once-in-a-generation event." The 1945 Government recognised "the benefits of a slower, steadier approach to reducing an even bigger debt…" than the debt we face today. Prosperity and fairness dictated that "Labour does need a credible and medium term plan to reduce the deficit and to reduce our level of national debt, but only once growth is fully secured and over a markedly longer period than George Osborne is currently planning." Such a plan requires "a careful balance between employment, spending, and taxation."

One complaint against such a policy is that government spending and borrowing will 'crowd out' the private investment we need for sustainable growth. Keynes called this the 'Treasury View'. It is inherent in the Government's plans and the OBR forecasts for investment. Ministers suggest that by getting out of the way, government will create the space for the private sector to recover.[36]

This argument about crowding out is based on a misunderstanding. When the economy is running near full capacity there is a case because increased government borrowing can push up interest rates. Since the private sector usually has to pay more than the Government to borrow, the cost of investment rises too. Unless the extra government borrowing is for investment that has better prospects than private sector plans, there can be a problem and the economy's long term productivity is hit. During a deep recession the situation is different. It is precisely because private sector activity has dropped that it is right for government to step in. If it had not done so in 2008 and 2009, we would have faced a depression rather than a deep recession.

There are, however, serious problems with simply maintaining a large deficit and hoping that growth will pull the economy round. That growth will need to lead to higher tax revenues, so tax policy is important. Taxes will also need to be higher or spending growth reduced when growth is established to pay down government debt that does not rise and fall naturally over the cycle; the structural deficit. So a credible plan is essential.

To that end, Labour has to demonstrate that in government it will ensure government spending is well-directed. In opposition, it should make an 'effective spending guarantee' to underline this commitment that spending will be proportional to the expected outcomes. All Labour frontbench members need to be clear how they would remodel the departments they shadow to be more effective at lower levels of spending growth. Ignore this and we will not appear serious about our economic policy, especially since spending is likely to have been slashed by the next election. The debate here will be less about what would we cut and more about our spending priorities versus the Conservatives, and our approach to overall spending levels.

It is also essential that market confidence that the deficit is under control is maintained, we must know why we are running a deficit, and government stimulus should be focused.

The bond markets

Chancellor George Osborne said in his 2010 Budget statement that "Questions that were asked about the liquidity and solvency of banking systems are now being asked of the liquidity and solvency of some of the Governments that stand behind those banks. I do not want those questions ever to be asked of this country."[37] The mix of Tory ideology and establishment panic at the time has been considered above. Osborne contends that a loss of market confidence would lead to a sharp rise in interest rates.

James Carville joked: "If there is reincarnation, I want to come back as the bond market. You can intimidate anybody."

This would happen because the price of UK government debt (bonds known as gilts) would fall. It suited Osborne to highlight this risk but bond markets cannot be ignored. This is the case even if bond investors eventually are proved wrong. James Carville, Bill Clinton's campaign strategist, famously joked: "If there is reincarnation, I want to come back as the bond market. You can intimidate anybody."

Bond markets matter to Governments because Governments borrow by issuing new bonds. The price they can sell new bonds for is determined by the rate of interest investors demand for lending to the Government. The higher the interest rate (or yield), the lower the price of the bond.[38] Normally, government bonds are the lowest risk bonds available, which means their interest rates are usually low compared to corporate bonds. The risk of default is usually regarded as low. A Government has access to the resources of the entire country so unless the economy is in a total mess it can always pay interest payments and the principal amount back. Where a country controls its own currency, it can also print money to pay back its debt (at the risk of higher inflation). Most government bonds have high credit ratings (the highest from Standard and Poor is AAA). The higher the risk of default, the lower the credit rating. Credit ratings tend to follow investor perceptions about the credit worthiness of a country. If investors are worried that debt is not being controlled sufficiently, they perceive that the risk of default has risen (even if it is still very low) or that the risk is higher that Governments will use inflation to erode the real value of their debt. Alternatively, higher government debt means more bonds being issued, which might lead to lower prices unless demand for bonds also increases. In these circumstances, bond interest rates (yields) can rise and with them, the cost of borrowing further. This is what Greece, Ireland, Portugal, Spain, and Italy experienced over the summer.

Investors can be wrong: Ed Balls notes that Churchill returned the UK to the Gold Standard in 1925 "on the grounds there was no credible alternative which the financial markets would support."[39] The financial markets were very wrong. The economist JK Galbraith later warned of the dangers of 'conventional wisdom'.[40] There is currently a conventional wisdom that deficits must be cut quickly. Yet ultimately investors want to be confident that government borrowing will not spiral out of control, requiring larger adjustments later, as in Greece. That is not an unreasonable demand and policy must be set in that light. That points to a clear plan to control debt but also to a policy which encourages growth. If debt is reduced too quickly (cutting government spending, raising taxes) the economy may struggle to recover. This would lead to lower tax revenues and hence upward pressure on borrowing. At this point, markets will begin to fear a scenario in which debt is rising but growth is falling. Bond investors can change their minds quicker than Governments can change their policies.

In the negotiations over the US debt ceiling, the Obama administration illustrated what happens when governments focus on growth and ignore deficits. If you are not credible on deficits, credibility will be forced upon you. If you do not have a plan of your own to control government borrowing, someone else will provide you with one, and it might not be a plan you will like. So it was that an administration focused on stimulating growth in a faltering economy agreed to large spending cuts with little if any room to use the tax system to mitigate the regressive nature of deficit cutting. Moreover, investors did not believe the spending cuts were credible (for one thing, it was not clear how much spending would be cut and much relied on further negotiations in Congress) and neither did rating agency Standard and Poors, which downgraded US Government debt from AAA to AA+ with a negative outlook. Better thinking might have produced a credible plan which did not threaten growth.

Bond market investors will look at both the annual deficit (the difference between spending and tax revenue) and the net debt/GDP ratio. Under Labour, the latter ratio was forecast to rise to almost 75 per cent (a higher ratio had been feared during the crisis); the current forecast peak is 70.9 per cent in 2013/14 The economists Reinhart and Rogoff find that deficits higher than 90 per cent of GDP are linked with lower growth rates; below 90 per cent there is little if any relationship. This level is becoming a benchmark for markets and policy-makers[41] but one which few wish governments to exceed.

The risk which became evident over the summer is that lack of credibility on deficit reduction leads markets to force governments to produce stringent austerity measures which themselves risk growth. Lower growth means lower tax revenue, which prompts markets again to pressure Governments into more extreme measures. The downward spiral leads to a lack of confidence in bond markets. If they effectively close, a Government has to print money, borrow from the IMF, or, if it is in the eurozone, borrow from European Union institutions.

Investment

It seems that every fiscal stimulus is made in the name of Keynes. This does him – and us – a disservice. Keynes' general point was that in a slump some activity is better than none, however inefficient it may be. Government has a role to stimulate activity which, via a multiplier effect, can ripple through the economy. It does not necessarily follow that all the measures aimed at helping consumers were Keynesian – or appropriate. Keynes's prescription was to keep long term interest rates low and for government to step in by promoting investment spending, which can fluctuate over the economic cycle.[42] Private sector investment is dependent not only on interest rates but on businesses' confidence in the future. Investment dropped sharply in the recession, for example, reflecting lower confidence in the future and tight credit conditions (many companies could not borrow even if they wanted to). There is a strong case for government investment to fill the gap, or at least targeted spending which prompts businesses to invest . Deficit-funded investment spending boosts immediate growth and also adds to the economy's productive potential in future (eg a new railway line lowers business costs).

Any deficit-for-growth policy therefore has to focus on investment spending, even at the expense of current spending, and it can ultimately fund itself through higher long term growth. Unfortunately, Labour's budget plans showed planned government investment falling after the initial stimulus, in absolute terms and as a proportion of GDP. Labour should reconsider its approach to investment and should even advocate spending cuts or a deficit in excess of Alistair Darling's plans (adjusted for subsequent economic performance) to pay for higher capital spending.

It may be that youth unemployment is a factor (but not an excuse) behind the rioting and looting over the summer.

The investment approach is not the whole answer however. It is not clear to what extent Keynes would have advocated it. Government spending on investment can push up prices and incomes in some sectors (eg construction) and lead to imbalances.[43] Government-inspired investment can be poorly devised and misdirected, with long time lags. During the recession between the wars, arguments for spending on public works were initially confounded by the paucity of 'shovel-ready' projects:[44] the same is true today. We seem to have forgotten that government investment spending cannot be turned on and off like a tap. This is why Governments often resort to trying to boost consumer spending during downturns. Even that method does not work instantly and is dependent on the level of consumer confidence and to some extent the willingness of households to increase their debt further. The effects can be uncertain and inefficient especially in terms of the number of people kept in work, which is surely our ultimate goal (in other words, though it may achieve something, measured against its aims it may be similar to wasteful spending). Arguably, Keynes himself was most concerned with measures that had a direct impact on unemployment, whether in recessions or expansions.[45] So investment spending has an important place but is not the complete answer.

Employment

A better approach is for government to fund employment and ultimately to be an employer of last resort. This avoids the problems of delays and inefficiencies in government spending. It is also clearly consistent with Labour values; it keeps people participating in the economy. This is not the same as expanding unemployment welfare payments in recession, as in the United States.[46] As a recession bites, unemployment rises. Rather than simply make a transfer payment from those in work to those out of work, government employs people directly (or funds employment) at a limited rate. This could be work in the voluntary sector or in key parts of the public sector where existing skills can be applied or limited training is required. It should be combined with a large increase in training provision. It is more productive generally for people to be doing something rather than nothing. It is also more productive for individuals themselves. As Professor David Blanchflower noted while a member of the Bank of England's Monetary Policy Committee, unemployment has serious psychological and social implications:

Unemployment has undeniably adverse effects on those unfortunate to experience it. A range of evidence indicates that unemployment tends to be associated with malnutrition, illness, mental stress, depression, increases in the suicide rate, poor physical health in later life and reductions in life expectancy. However, there is also a wider social aspect. Many studies find a strong relationship between crime rates and unemployment, particularly for property crime. Sustained unemployment while young, especially of long duration, is especially damaging. By preventing labour market entrants from gaining a foothold in employment, sustained youth unemployment may reduce their productivity. Those that suffer youth unemployment tend to have lower incomes and poorer labour market experiences in later decades. Unemployment while young creates permanent scars rather than temporary blemishes.[47]

It may be that current high levels of youth unemployment are a contributory factor (but not an excuse) behind the outbreaks of rioting and looting over the summer.

Labour moved a step towards more direct employment policies with its Future Jobs Fund. As its 2010 manifesto outlined:

No young person in Britain should be long-term unemployed: those out of work for six months or more will be guaranteed employment or training through the £1 billion Future Jobs Fund, with mandatory participation after ten months. The fund will support 200,000 jobs. All those who are long-term unemployed for two years will be guaranteed a job placement, which they will be required to take up or have their benefits cut.

Germany adopted a policy of subsidising jobs during the downturn. Neither country experienced the rise in unemployment it had expected. In part this was due to government policy. Many businesses also appear to have looked through the sudden tightening of bank credit and hoarded labour rather than made people redundant (with business confidence helped by government focused on stimulus rather than ill-timed austerity). UK firms saw profit margins drop dramatically as they did this and then bounce as demand picked up. If recovery is sluggish, they may decide to maintain margins by cutting (labour) costs. That points also to a taxation policy which rewards employment as much as is practicable. An active employment policy is necessary. A policy such as the Future Jobs Fund should be a permanent feature of a Labour Government.

Longer term

Longer term, the debate about public finances needs to be put in the context of the needs we will have over the next few years and decades. In particular, an ageing population will have particular needs and climate change may require high expenditure (for example, in dealing with more natural disasters). Whether funded privately or publicly, the economy will need to be more productive in order to meet the challenges (or we will all be much poorer). The task of promoting genuine sustainable growth will become more urgent, for without it we will not be able to afford the services we expect to be available. Some public services (eg nursing homes) will need to be mutualised to ensure people have a clear stake, visibility on future funding, and ownership of the outcomes. A 'whole economy' approach to public finances needs to be adopted, with fiscal policy kept under close control but judged by its role in promoting the level of investment the economy requires.

At the same time we must avoid a past mistake, which was to think of public finances and the economy as static systems in which it is simple to raise a tax here or cut spending there. In reality, the economy is incredibly dynamic. People and companies respond to price incentives. So we should regard long term predictions of government spending with some suspicion. For example, an ageing population will change the dynamics of care provision, which may provide opportunities for social entrepreneurs to enter that market to build more and better quality homes (let's not forget that people living longer is a nice problem to have). Limits on government health spending may risk the nation's health, but may also prompt enterprising companies to find lower cost methods of producing drugs and equipment.

Deficits – conclusion

Advocates of maintaining deficit financing need to be clear what exactly the deficit is for and how it will be used. Financial crises produce large deficits (government debt has expanded an average 86 per cent in major crises globally since the Second World War).[48] History suggests there is time to address them but there has to be a clear plan and progress, otherwise Governments can face sudden capital outflows as market sentiment turns. Economic credibility is vital. Stimulus measures should focus on building the productive potential of the economy. Rather than promote forms of consumption, government should focus on maintaining investment and employment.

In the longer term, a clearer 'whole economy' approach should be adopted towards fiscal policy, with some services mutualised to promote greater transparency and accountability. An economy needs both measures to encourage growth and a credible plan for ensuring public finances are in a sustainable position. The two must go together. The time for short term growth fixes is over. A pro-employment policy coupled with targeted measures to promote investment is required, together with a policy on deficits which gives everyone, both taxpayers and market investors, confidence in the future.

5. INDUSTRIAL STRATEGY

A proactive industrial strategy is not the easy answer many seem to believe it to be. It has its place but we must be clear about what we are trying to achieve and it must be based on sound economics. Unfortunately, political pressures too often take precedence.

Calls for a new industrial strategy can often be heard from the left. We feel instinctively that it is a good thing. An economy which makes things and where government does not leave companies abandoned to the ravages of a free market is surely the ideal foundation for a good society. The problem is that progressives have little idea what such a 21st century strategy would look like. Moreover, they have not learned the lessons of the past.

We need to re-imagine the relationship between the state and the private sector. In broad terms, we should aim to create an environment in which we reduce business uncertainty as much as possible. That will mean a simple and stable tax environment and a renewed focus on incentives. Our focus on power will lead to proactive help to ensure companies get access to finance and a strengthened competition policy. Economic power held by individuals will be increased by a renewed commitment to skills.

Government intervention used to have a bad name and in general it should continue to do so. We too soon forget the disasters of the 1970s nationalisations. It is easy to blame the Thatcher Governments for destroying the industrial heartlands of our economy. Indeed, we should not underestimate the devastation caused by Conservative ideology, especially since we have a Government run by her admirers today. There were other factors in play which could have been addressed differently – economic policy does matter. As the UK produced oil from the North Sea, so oil demand from overseas bid up the pound against other currencies, making our industrial exports more expensive in world markets. An alternative policy would have invested oil revenues overseas rather than pay for tax cuts, thereby lowering the exchange rate, boosting exports, and generating income in future years (or there could have been more focus on investment in the domestic economy). The experience of the 1970s helped prevent this as a political option.

Too many taxpayer pounds were wasted on companies that should have been restructured or gone to the wall years previously. Experiences in the 1970s demonstrate how difficult government intervention can be. Bernard Donoughue, in his Downing Street Diaries,[49] describes the negotiations aimed at saving a Chrysler plant in Scotland in 1975. The Government ended up agreeing to commit millions to a plan it did not believe was economically viable, so strong were the political pressures.

The financial crisis brought intervention back into fashion. The banks benefited from a variety of interventions, including nationalisation, which dwarfed previous examples in other industries. As the economy plunged into recession, Labour changed tack on business policy.

Peter Mandelson outlined the new approach in December 2008 as the new Secretary of State for Business, in a lecture entitled 'A new industrial activism'.[50] It focused more on pointing to a new approach than providing details about how it would work. He was clear about the mistakes of the 1970s, an in this respect insisted the Government's approach had not changed: "Whatever the short term decisions we make on transitional assistance for businesses faced with the extraordinary strains of the downturn, in the long term there is no propping up unviable companies or running businesses from Whitehall. No heavy-handed state. No backing away from free trade or open markets or the discipline of competition."

While Mandelson's rhetoric appeared to herald a new phase in progressive politics it suffered from the same problems that Labour faced when intervening in the

The 2010 Labour manifesto lacked a clear and simple explanation of what Labour planned to do and why.

financial system. Political ideology, and not just policy, was being remade as we went along. As calls for intervention increased, it was difficult to develop the overarching economic narrative. A Government paper '*Going for Growth: Our Future Prosperity*' was produced in 2010 but its lack of substantial content demonstrated this problem.

This was also seen in the 2010 Labour manifesto, which, despite some potentially attractive business policies, lacked a clear and simple explanation of what Labour planned to do and why. There was no shortage of programmes proposed that were intended to transform the economy. Labour went into the last General Election trumpeting a new 'UK Finance for Growth Fund' that aimed to match £4bn of public money with private funds 'to channel equity to business.' That itself contained a 'Growth Capital Fund', which focused on small and medium sized enterprises (SMEs) 'which need capital injections of between £2 and £10 million'. Labour also announced an 'Innovation Investment Fund' focused on high tech firms, new investment in nuclear and renewable industries would be assisted by a Strategic Investment Fund, university research through a 'Higher Education Innovation Fund' and a new 'University Enterprise Capital Fund', and regional development through a new 'regional growth fund' combined with increased ministerial intervention. There were many funds, but little money. We made a classic mistake by focusing more on policies we thought would appeal to business than on the overall narrative.

The current Government is experiencing a similar problem. It was much criticised for delays to its white paper on growth and the measures in its 2011 Budget were the usual mixture of half-hearted measures. It remains to be seen whether its next set of plans will appear convincing.

Mandelson allowed for direct government intervention to support business in the short term during periods of difficulty. Yet when businesses are in trouble it is *almost always* claimed to be due to some apparent transitory issue. Once government intervention is a possibility the political pressure can build very quickly. We saw this with government subsidies to motorists who scrapped their old cars and bought new models, in many cases probably incurring more debt as they did so.[51]

Short term help aside, there is a case for an ongoing role for the state to help the business sector. The aim should be to encourage greater productivity, increase the productive potential of the economy, and provide a long term framework where there is market failure, such as with the threat of climate change.

A 21st Century industrial activism needs to start not with what government can do to help but with the incentives that are embedded in our economy. Rather than attempt to fund an activity, government should think about how better to encourage an outcome. For example, should we put public money into low carbon technologies or should we fund tax breaks for reductions in greenhouse gas emissions? If businesses are confident the tax system is stable, they and financiers can take the risk and find their own solutions. More importantly, should we ensure the pricing mechanism for fossil fuels properly incorporates a cost of carbon and allow it to signal investment opportunities to entrepreneurs to provide low cost energy?[52]

The role of incentives and the need for a clear and simple tax system must be understood by the Left. Let us accept as a principle that we will not attempt to second guess business decisions. We will let business take the risks within a stable economic policy framework. If a business fails, the owners will take the loss but the next Labour Government will have put in place more support for employees aimed at sustaining their skill levels and getting them back into work. If we want to increase research and development, let us resolve that our first step will be to help businesses plan for the long term and have access to finance, rather than play around with tax credits. We will also provide a stable framework of sustained infrastructure investment, raising the economy's productive potential and giving businesses more certainty for their own plans. The results will be hard to model, but economic forecasting has a poor track record anyway. What matters is whether the economic environment encourages business confidence and that policy does not add unnecessarily to the uncertainties businesses already face.

There is a role for intervention but it must be long term in nature and removed from political pressures. The German investment bank, KfW, offers an attractive model. Founded as part of the post war Marshall Plan, it does not fund business investment directly but it acts as a second tier bank which backs commercial bank loans to business. These can help start-ups, boost the balance sheets of small and medium sized enterprises, and help fund green energy projects. If the business plan appears economically viable, KfW will take on some of the credit risk of a loan, thereby encouraging bank lending and keeping interest rates low. Its own borrowing is backed by the German Government, which enables it to sustain a AAA credit rating and borrow on favourable terms.

A British equivalent, a British Investment Bank, would require a clear mission statement and protection from political pressure. The lending criteria would have to be robust and clear. Over time, such a bank could become a British institution yet one which was dynamic and considered itself accountable to future generations.[53] Some sort of national investment bank is not a novel suggestion. The challenge is to develop an institution fit for the 21st Century. Sometimes calls for a national investment bank appear to imply that it would instantly channel funds to manufacturing businesses which are currently starved of investment. For it to work, it will have to be robust in the way it assesses potential borrowers, it will serve all sectors of the economy, and it will need to be immune from popularist political pressure while avoiding capture by neoliberalism. All this will take time to develop. The national investment bank will need to have its own culture but not be dominated by a City banking perspective.

The small business sector is lauded in politics and there is never a bad word said about it. Few politicians dare mention the fact that while our small and medium size enterprises play a vital role and generate a large number of jobs, the quality of businesses can be quite variable. Many SMEs are innovative and well run but it is not a given that all SMEs are a 'good thing'. Small businesses can be highly dependent upon management quality (as employees of poor managers, often unfamiliar with the benefits of trade union membership,

We need to invest still further in each other – the human capital of UK plc.

know only too well) and during a recession poor financial controls can be revealed. Recovering markets may not always help. For example, if a company is not managing its working capital (stocks, debtors, creditors) properly, it could be receiving strong growth in its order book but be unable to purchase the parts needed to produce final products for its customers. With bank lending tight and perhaps existing borrowing already at high levels, a small business could easily sink or simply limp on.

Small businesses are also likely to have a limited idea about how to take advantage of a lower exchange rate. A British Investment Bank could also help fund consultancy services for SMEs. Measures such as these can help improve the relative power of SMEs and could encourage banks to take a longer term approach to lending.

We take for granted the assertion that banks are being too slow to lend to business and this may be true to a large extent. However, while larger companies appear to have very healthy balance sheets, many smaller firms may still be carrying an uncomfortable amount of debt; with an uncertain outlook who would lend to them? It might make more sense for everyone for banks to convert the debt to equity, find some good managers and encourage a few mergers. A British Investment Bank might be able to help this happen.

Small businesses might also benefit from a redesigned competition policy designed to prevent undue accumulation of monopoly power.

There is another area where government intervention is often demanded: skills. We need to invest still further in each other – the human capital of UK plc. Labour made great strides in education investment and this needs to be maintained. We need not simply technologists who can perform highly skilled tasks; we need more engineers in all fields. A highly educated and adaptable working population increases the incentives for businesses to invest.

During a recession or sharp financial shock, companies can get into difficulties and lay off workers. The risk in doing so for the economy is that those people's skills could be lost. This is also a risk for the companies, which may be one reason why firms hoarded labour more during the recent recession than previously. When it does happen however, the state should intervene. As well as acting as employer of last resort, there could be a whole new focus on education and training. It is here where there is surely more scope for work with trade unions as we seek to keep people in work.

Would this new focus exclude government intervention in the business sector during a recession? It would better define it. During a shortage of credit and sudden drop in confidence brought about by a financial crisis, there would be a good case for intervention designed to help companies manage cashflow and prevent collapse. It should not be aimed at distorting markets for products and services – other measures to raise general demand should help. Strong political judgement is required to keep the intervention short term. If it takes place within a new policy framework such as that described above this should be easier. It should also take place with open markets, with Britain fulfilling its role as a vibrant trading nation.[54]

Well-run businesses also tend to be virtuous businesses. By encouraging a stronger business sector we can get nearer to the society we hope for. Business is not an add-on, it is a fundamental part of human life and an expression of human creativity. A New Economic Fabianism would see government working to ensure everyone is involved in economic life. A more equal access to investment finance would be promoted alongside a higher commitment to ongoing training for people, with a backstop of a job guarantee. These aims will require some robust decisions by Labour in government, because there will be vested interests to challenge and new ways of thinking to adopt.

We need the following:

- a simple and stable **tax system for business**, which helps to reduce uncertainty and promote a more stable economy;
- bold and simple **economic incentives** preferred to government picking business solutions;
- a government focus on **infrastructure** investment;
- a **British Investment Bank** with a clear mandate to serve the nation using robust investment criteria;
- a robust **competition policy**;
- a new **focus on skills**.

6. FINANCIAL REFORM AND REBALANCING

As a matter of economic necessity banking must be reformed. Too-systemic-to-fail banks represent a clear and present danger to the UK economy. But Labour must learn to love the City again too.

" **I** have no idea what is going on in the banks, and I'm a banking analyst," remarked an investment analyst to a meeting of fund managers I attended in the autumn of 2008. Lehman Brothers had collapsed the previous month. It is difficult now to describe the sensation felt by many investment professionals as the foundations of the financial sector were shaken, though we have had a similar experience in the summer of 2011. It was no surprise therefore that we had the deepest recession since the 1930s. The crisis exposed the fragile foundations on which our economic system was built. Those foundations remain weak, exacerbated by the flawed conventional wisdom about deficits.

Financial crises are more common than we might think. They are frequent occurrences. The UK alone has experienced four banking crises since 1945 and twelve since 1800.[55] They are a natural feature of capitalism, though they are not often globally systemic in nature as in 2008. They normally follow a period of stability, when confidence rises, asset price bubbles emerge, and regulation and procedures begin to be relaxed. Eventually, the level of speculation and borrowing in the system becomes so high a 'Minsky Moment' occurs when a part of the financial system becomes a giant Ponzi scheme.[56] Collapse follows.

Labour needs to think afresh. It must avoid welcoming every proposal for taxing the banks. It must recognise that it is better to promote a sustainable banking sector than turn banks away. More widely, it needs to rethink its approach to the financial sector.[57]

We tend to be in awe of our financial sector. Aside from the occasional crisis which can cancel out the gains very quickly (banks regularly find new ways to lose money) the City as a whole can be a major plus for the UK. We might want reform but we do not want to lose a competitive advantage in finance and a major source of tax revenue. It is possible to envisage a progressive City policy. It would promote the City as a place of ethical standards and work at least to prevent institutions harming the common good. It would reward enterprise and prevent the accumulation of excessive market power.

Despite recent events, the banking sector retains a large degree of power. Having opposed government intervention elsewhere in the economy, it demanded intervention for itself. A recipient of huge bailouts, government guarantees, and low interest rates, banking has passed judgement on governments whose finances had been brought low by its actions. It has responded to calls for reform with threats that banks and bankers will leave the country. Meanwhile remuneration has remained excessive, especially for a recession, and the bonus culture is returning.

The public sees banks acting more in the manner of ungrateful children than mature adults reflecting on their mistakes. The much-heralded Project Merlin, whereby government and banks attempted to bury the hatchet, seems to have been more of a bargaining exercise by the banks than an opportunity for mature reflection. The UK situation is not unique. Former IMF Chief Economist Simon Johnson argues that banks are financial oligarchs that must be broken up.[58] Not only do banks still 'not get it' with respect to public opinion but they still retain and use financial and political power, despite their role before and during the financial crisis. The UK Government has a particular responsibility to exercise leadership on this issue, given the global role played by our financial sector. Yet it is proving difficult for politicians to shake off the pre-crisis mindset.

Some of the financial reforms proposed are based on increasing tax revenue from the financial sector, via so-called 'Robin Hood' taxes. These include the Tobin Tax on currency transactions and various other taxes on financial transactions; bank levies, and a VAT-style tax on financial activities in general. Labour introduced a bank bonus levy, which raised more revenue than expected because the banks increased their payouts rather than reduce bonus payments. The aim with these taxes is to cream off revenue from a buoyant financial sector and redress the imbalance in the economy by redistributing the funds to other parts of the economy, especially in the case of the Tobin Tax to the global poor.

Banking taxes could be used to pay down government debt in preparation for the next banking crisis. A similar proposal is to charge an insurance levy on banks, linked to concerns that regulators have about financial leverage and asset price inflation.[59] Since a bail-out would cost the taxpayer, it seems reasonable to charge banks some sort of insurance premium, if the risk of moral hazard could be avoided.

The problem with revenue-raising reforms is that they do little to address the fundamental problem that financial crises are endemic to capitalism. Some taxes, such as the bank levy, seem more designed to punish banks for the recent disaster than prevent a future occurrence. The challenge is to prevent crises becoming systemic and if a systemic event does occur, to halt its progress and protect people from its effects

The calls during the crisis for new standards of behaviour in financial markets now seem like echoes from another time. A structural reform is required. The separation of banking activities between utility banking and more risky ventures would put barriers in the way of systemic failures. The problem is not that banks can be 'too big to fail' but that, as Bank of England Governor Mervyn King noted, they can be 'too important to fail'. Separation of banking activities, combined with effective regulation, would minimise this risk and clearly define the extent to which government deposit guarantees apply. Advocates of reform of this kind include King,[60] the economist John Kay,[61] and on the Left the Christian Socialist Movement.[62] In the US, former Federal Reserve Chairman Paul Volcker had some of his proposals on separation written into law by Congress.

The Government's Independent Commission on Banking (ICB) final report proposed that systemically important banks should have an equity-to-asset ratio of 10 per cent in addition to loss-absorbing debt – a tighter capital requirement against future disasters than the sector consensus under the new Basel III agreement on bank regulation. It also suggested that retail bank operations should be ring-fenced within larger banking groups. It is doubtful whether these measures would withstand the fast-moving dynamics of major crisis or individual bank run. Depositors may not wait to see if the higher level of capital held by a bank in trouble was sufficient. The ICB's final report, published in September, will need to be studied to see whether it fully addresses this concern and whether it gives fuller consideration to the case for separation of banking activities. Stricter regulation is on its way but is untested and over time will be subject to erosion. Clear separation of banking activities would answer these concerns. In addition, the market for banking services should not be dominated by a few large institutions. A more competitive, and perhaps more regionally focused, banking market would contrast with the accumulation of market power under the present rather odd version of capitalism that we tolerate.

Labour has expressed limited enthusiasm for radical bank reform, and it does not appear to have made a submission to the ICB. In government, despite having organised an historic bailout of the banks, Labour's message was that it was all too difficult to attempt major reform of the financial sector. It was another example of how Labour's political ideology had yet to catch up with reality.

Reform of the City must go wider than preventing another banking crisis. There must be more incentives to encourage longer term investment. However, longer term investment is not necessarily a good in itself; after all, many long term investments are simply short term investments gone wrong. And mistakes can be made longer term too. Ultimately it comes down to management quality and the incentives in the system. Good quality management is highly valuable but difficult to define. A well-run company will tend to be ethically run as well as being profitable. Management will pay attention to the basics, from a focus on cashflow to investment in its people. It will be willing to take risks but to achieve sustainable profit growth and not, for example, simply bigger scale for its own sake.

The problem is that the incentives in the system work against good management. The short-termism of investors is often blamed. In a world of hedge funds and proprietary trading desks, short term trading certainly does take place. This can damage a company if investor sentiment turns suddenly, though at other times trading helps provide a liquid market for shares. Investors will also sell shares if their trust in management's ability to deliver falls. Trust is crucial for long term investment. This is especially the case since financial modelling has little predictive power beyond the short term. Changes in interest rates and inflation, new innovations or overall levels of demand cannot be predicted with certainty and the discounted cashflow models often used are highly sensitive to analysts' assumptions.[63] So while the figures must stack up on any investment project, other factors are important and for investors much depends on the trust they have in management judgement and ability. A reformed City will place more emphasis on the role of fund managers as stewards on behalf of the owners of assets, often pension funds. Pension funds need to see themselves as owners of a slice of UK (or World) plc. For example, global action on banks might be more effective if pension funds around the world (which part own banks) were able to come to a common view. This would answer bank threats to move jurisdiction.

Another incentive is remuneration. Executive pay is often excessive. Pay levels have lost touch with reality and put executive directors (of listed companies) in a different dimension to most people; in 2006-10, a period when most peoples incomes were under pressure, pay rose an average of 24.5 per cent for FTSE 100 company directors.[64] Company remuneration policies are normally complex and not easy for investors to scrutinise. Performance targets are often too easily attained but are usually based on relatively short term earnings growth or the company's share price performance compared to its peers. This risks distorting management priorities. Indeed, it is not clear to what extent pay should be linked to performance. The link between the two is not strong and besides investors should not want to employ chief executives who would work less if paid a bit less; the expectation is that a chief executive will work as hard as possible in the role.

UK investors can vote on remuneration but these votes are advisory only and refer to existing policies. So-called long term incentive plans also go to a vote. A reformed City would include simple remuneration policies with any performance element being genuinely long term (eg through an average economic cycle). Binding shareholder approval would be required before implementation. We should go further still. Concerned as we are with abuse of economic power at the top, this must be combined with our main concern lower down the pay scale. This is truly about sharing the proceeds of growth. The ratio of highest to lowest paid in companies has been growing; the ratio itself says much about the way a company is run.

Companies should be required to publish the salary ratio of the highest to the lowest ten per cent. Investment institutions should have to report publicly their reasons for backing pay schemes with a ratio higher than a defined level.[65]

The financial crisis exposed a dramatic mispricing of risk. Most financial models proved inadequate to the task of predicting accurately the probability of the events of 2007-9 occurring. The risks were compounded by gearing – the use of debt to magnify returns. Gearing can work in reverse when prices fall. A greater emphasis on equity investment might force financial institutions to assess risk more realistically and the tax advantages of debt finance should be reviewed once more. The City's ability to channel funds where they are needed should be recognised however. Larger companies are able to go straight to the market for debt funding rather than borrow directly from banks.

A reformed City would also be more open to different types of company. This might enable new forms of cooperatives to raise funds for investment without compromising their identity or being dependent upon banks.

Simply downplaying finance will not do for Labour. It is not good enough to simply express anger at the banks. There is limited political gain in it and besides, we need to be looking to the future. Wishing too that finance will suddenly become willing to fund all sorts of civil society projects is just being wishful and is actually beside the point. We must recognise that the City contains a range of institutions other than banks. Some, such as the pension fund managers, may have similar ideas on reform and a similar attitude towards banks. Labour should talk to them and discuss their ideas.

A virtuous City is certainly within reach, given there are many good people working in finance. A Labour Government would work with them. An effective financial sector is a good thing, because it can attract finance and financial services are an area of comparative advantage for the UK. Labour would challenge the undue accumulation of financial power, in the UK and overseas, because if it does not we will risk a further crisis and besides it can lead to inequality in a manner which offends many peoples view of social justice. Economic power will be more fairly distributed, for example through more appropriate remuneration policies. Tough decisions again will be required by Labour in government, both in the decision to engage and in promoting the reforms it wants to see. The hope is that post the crisis, the City will understand that the approach described here is in its long term interests.

A progressive City would...

- separate utility banking from more risky banking;
- contain a number of lower risk, more regionally focused, banks and banking divisions of larger institutions;
- respond to government incentives encouraging longer term investment;
- further reform executive remuneration schemes;
- be less dependent on debt;
- be renowned for a high standard of ethical behaviour and transparency.

These aims are designed to enable the market system to work better, unfettered by the accumulation of market power; progressive outcomes can then occur. To get anywhere near achieving these objectives, Labour has to learn to love the City again, but in a more enduring and honest relationship – and with a City reformed.

7. THE POLITICAL ECONOMY WE NEED

The Left will make little headway if it simply works out what it would do now. To win power in future elections in the UK and across Europe it must be relevant to people's aspirations for the future.

Maintaining a high deficit indefinitely, promoting intervention wherever we feel the market has failed, and making things tougher for the banks are not the easy solutions some on the Left believe them to be. Our responses to these ideas will shed light on our underlying economic thinking and we have to get that right. These ideas relate to the questions we face today. While we might at some point face a snap General Election, our thinking has to embrace the concerns people will have in 2015 as they look ahead to 2020 and beyond.

If the coalition Government is successful, the deficit and overall public debt levels will be on downward tracks by the next General Election in accordance with its fiscal rules. It will have survived pushing through the major spending cuts and welfare reforms. Looking ahead, it will consider what relief it can offer. If the two parties campaign separately, it is likely the Conservatives will emphasise tax cuts while the Liberal Democrats will include some additional element of spending.

If economic growth disappoints, the Government may find itself in political difficulties. Spending cuts will have gone through but unemployment will remain stubborn. A 'Plan B' would increase the deficit; this is permitted under the new fiscal rules but there is limited room for manoeuvre and it would represent failure. The Government will look to blame external circumstances or, still, Labour's supposed legacy. For Labour, the scary thing is that people might well believe them.

In either of these circumstances, Labour will not win the election if it campaigns on what it would have done over the previous five years. It has to answer the concerns people will have about the *following* five years. It is impossible to predict what economic growth will be in two years' time, let alone what the economy will look like in 2015 and beyond. We can begin to focus on what the long term trends might be, the values that will underpin Labour economic management and what that would mean in practice.

The underlying foundations will be an aim to build an economy that works and that works for everyone rather than a few individuals, businesses, or banks. As people look ahead to their career or education prospects, they need to have confidence in the future. It may be some time before we return to the gentle days where growth was steady and inflation low, but we know the foundations were weak across the rich economies. Now, we need to be confident our employers can think longer term, that economies will not be derailed again by bank failures, and that in a changing world we can acquire the skills we need to get on.

That will only come about in a society with a clearer sense of the common good, where people have more say over the things which influence their lives and are impatient with privilege and unfair accumulation of power. But this is not some dream. If we are clear about our approach to public finances, if we focus on encouraging investment and guaranteeing employment, and if we promote financial reform, we will be acting in a way that helps our market economy function without the distortions of past years. We will have a progressive economy.

Our next manifesto must have a clear message running through it rather than a jumble of (often very good) policies. The battleground of the next election is not yet clear. However, Labour must build a message of economic hope on a foundation of restored economic credibility.

Our message for Britain should be that we will focus on building an economy in which all can participate and where values matter. To do this, a Labour Government will underwrite education, training and employment while investing to improve the productive potential of a dynamic economy. It will guarantee to put people first and combine this with better managed spending and a reformed financial system. It will act on the people's behalf by opposing undue accumulation of economic power. Finally, Labour's message has to be one of investment in our future, with government working alongside people for a better future for them and their families.

1. In *Beyond the Crash* (2010), Gordon Brown does recount how he made an attempt to improve global mechanisms for promoting financial stability but regrets he did not push harder.
2. http://www.ipsos-mori.com/researchpublications/research archive/poll.aspx?oItemID=22&view=wide
3. http://www.ipsos-mori.com/researchpublications/research archive/poll.aspx?oItemId=2375&view=wide
4. The public finances under Labour, Institute for Fiscal Studies January 2009.
5. The coalition may discover this as it applies its own two fiscal rules: to balance the cyclically-adjusted current budget by the end of a rolling five year period and to see net debt falling in 2015/16.
6. In 2007/8.
7. Which he recounts in *Beyond the Crash* (2010).
8. "All financial innovation involves, in one form or another, the creation of debt secured in greater or lesser adequacy by real assets." *A short history of financial euphoria*, JK Galbraith (1990).
9. See *Capitalism 4.0*, Anatole Kaletsky (2010).
10. Institute for Fiscal Studies Election Briefing Note No.12, 2010. The Conservatives and Liberal Democrats also left billions in spending cuts unspecified going into the General Election.
11. Whatever the economics, the state of bond markets in April and May 2010 was one of high anxiety. Without a statement, a Labour

Government would have waited passively for the next market mood swing. I am not suggesting Darling needed to alter his plans fundamentally, aside from adjusting for lower growth.

12 Which goes to show how little value economic growth forecasts actually have.

13 The Conservative Party did not think so at the time, since it supported Labour's spending plans.

14 "I think that we should have been looking much harder at what was happening to the 'squeezed middle', which was a problem that actually started in 2004', interview, *Progress* magazine, September 2011.

15 For example, see YouGov's economy tracker http://today.yougov. co.uk/sites/today.yougov.co.uk/files/yg-archives-trackers-economy-310811.pdf

16 The financial crisis is comprehensively described in 'The Financial Crisis Inquiry Report of the National Commission on the Causes of the Financial and Economic Crisis in the United States' (2011).

17 We had reached a 'Minsky Moment', as described by UBS senior economic adviser George Magnus after the economist Hyman Minsky eg 'What this Minsky moment means', *Financial Times* 22 August 2007.

18 Speech by Mervyn King, Governor of the Bank of England, Civic Centre, Newcastle 25 January 2011.

19 If food and energy prices remain subdued we may see household discretionary income rise in 2012 as previous high prices and the VAT hike drop out of year on year comparisions.

20 Household debt in the Economic and fiscal outlook, Office for Budget Responsibility, 21 April 2011. The OBR assumes asset prices grow too, to enable more borrowing (though it rises as a proportion of income).

21 These points on inequality and relative poverty drawn from Poverty & Inequality in the UK, Rob Joyce, Institute for Fiscal Studies (2010).

22 The Resolution Foundation states that 11.1 million people can be defined as being on low or middle incomes, and who are broadly independent of state support.

23 'New study reveals effects of 'Great Recession' across OECD countries', IFS 12 September 2011. http://www.ifs.org.uk/publications/5671

24 'Complacent Cameron must leave the sidelines' *Financial Times*, 1 September 2011

25 This is Kaletsky's point.

26 In other words, a 'One Nation' progressive party.

27 See *Building the Good Society* by Jon Cruddas and Andrea Nahles published by Compass and Friedrich Ebert Stiftung.

28 "We need to fundamentally re-think the way we do things in the City." These were the words of a broker to me as we contemplated the chasm into which the financial sector was falling in 2008. He was talking about values rather than trading strategies.

29 For example, *Good value: reflections on money, morality and an uncertain world* by Stephen Green, then chairman of HSBC.

30 See especially *New Jerusalems: Labour Party and the economics of democratic socialism* by Elizabeth Durbin (1985).

31 *The Acquisitive Society*, RH Tawney (1920).

32 *Equality* (1931), RH Tawney.

33 Charles Moore, writing for the *Telegraph* web site ('I'm starting to think that the Left might actually be right'), suggested that the banking crisis showed that "it turns out – as the Left always claims – that a system purporting to advance the many has been perverted in order to enrich the few." We may not convince Mr Moore to support the Labour Party but our values are essential for an accessible market economy.

34 John Major's 'Cones Hotline' springs to mind as an example of policy failing to match rhetoric.

35 'The case against the growth deniers – how Labour can win the argument that there is an alternative', 27 August 2010.

36 Some talk about 'Ricardian equivalence' in this context. This is the proposition that households reduce their spending when government borrowing rises because they anticipate higher taxes later on to pay for it. There is much debate about whether this phenomenon exists and if it applies to an economy operating below full capacity.

37 Budget statement June 2010.

38 A gilt pays out a small amount each year known as a coupon and the total nominal value of the bond is paid at maturity. The yield, or interest rate, on a gilt is the annual return investors receive over the life of the bond if they buy it at the current market price. When bond prices fall, their yields rise and vice versa. A higher yield means the government has to pay more when it issues new debt.

39 27 August 2010.

40 *The Affluent Society*, JK Galbraith (1958).

41 http://www.voxeu.org/index.php?q=node/5395 Debt and Growth revisited, Reinhart & Rogoff (August 2010).

42 See *Keynes – the return of the master* by Robert Skidelsky (2009) for a succinct summary of Keynes' thinking.

43 See *Stablizing an Unstable Economy*, Hyman Minsky (1986).

44 See *Keynes* by Peter Clarke (2009) for an interesting account of the 1929 Macmillan Committee on public spending.

45 Pavlina Tcherneva makes a convincing case for this in 'Keynes approach to full employment: aggregate or effective demand?' Working paper no. 542, Levy Economics Institute of Bard College, August 2008.

46 Raghuram Rajan, in *Fault Lines* (2010), argues this is the implied pact the US government has with its people: a limited welfare net but ad hoc boosts to unemployment payments. He argues this creates uncertainty.

47 'What should be done about rising unemployment in the UK?' Open lecture at University of Sterling. David Blanchflower 25 February 2009.

48 This time is different, Reinhart and Rogoff (2009).

49 *Downing Street Diary – with Harold Wilson in No. 10* Bernard Donoughue (2005).

50 Speech to RSA 17 Dec 2008.

51 Philippe Legrain notes this discrepancy in his book *Aftershock* (2011).

52 While, separately, subsidising those most affected by an initially higher price for energy.

53 It should be held in trust by Parliament on behalf of the people rather than be a government agency or an unaccountable entity.

54 Which, incidentally, has implications for defence spending, but that is another issue altogether.

55 Reinhart and Rogoff This time is different 2009.

56 See Minsky (1986).

57 In contrast, I recall clearly my first Labour Party meeting, in 1994, when an activist joked that progress would be made by 'nuking' the City, along with the New York and Frankfurt financial districts. I reflected ruefully that I, and a number of school friends, worked there. His solution was somewhat drastic but the financial sector made a good job of bringing itself to the point of meltdown.

58 'The Quiet Coup', Simon Johnson, *Atlantic Magazine*, May 2009 http://www.theatlantic.com/magazine/archive/2009/05/the-quiet-coup/7364/4/

59 In a *Progress* web article in April 2008 I proposed a Financial Leverage Insurance Premium. The acronym FLIP accurately describes the banking sector's change in attitude towards government intervention when a bubble bursts. It is also one of the milder expressions a banker might use in such circumstances.

60 Speech to Scottish business organisations, Edinburgh, 20 October 2009.

61 Narrow Banking Centre for the Study of Financial Innovation September 2009: http://www.johnkay.com/2009/09/15/narrow-banking.

62 CSM was behind an Early Day Motion on this issue in 2009 and continues to push the idea. www.thecsm.org.uk

63 The value of an investment today can be estimated if we know or assume a growth rate of returns over its life, discounted by an interest rate. Vary either of these assumptions and the value can change significantly.

64 PIRC Annual Stewardship Review 2011.

65 A report commissioned by the Church Investors Group suggested a ratio of 75:1. Different types of business might need different criteria applied eg depending on the extent of outsourcing.

Further Reading

Essays in Persuasion, J M Keynes

General theory of Employment, Interest, and Money, J M Keynes

Stabilizing an Unstable Economy, Hyman Minsky (1986)

New Jerusalems: The Labour Party and the economics of democratic socialism, Elizabeth Durbin (1985)

A Short History of Financial Euphoria, J K Galbraith (1990)

Capitalism 4.0, Anatole Kaletsky (2010)

Keynes – The Return of the Master, Robert Skidelsky (2009)

Keynes, Peter Clarke (2009)

Fault Lines, Raghuram Rajan (2010)

Equality, R H Tawney

Them and Us, Will Hutton (2010)

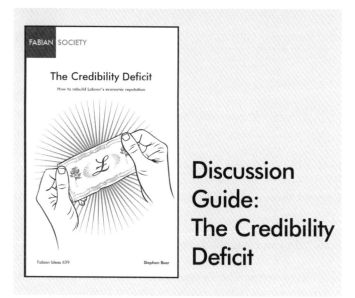

The Credibility Deficit
How to rebuild Labour's economic reputation

FABIAN SOCIETY

Fabian Ideas 629   Stephen Beer

Discussion Guide: The Credibility Deficit

How to use this Discussion Guide

The guide can be used in various ways by Fabian Local Societies, local political party meetings and trade union branches, student societies, NGOs and other groups.

■ You might hold a discussion among local members or invite a guest speaker – for example, an MP, academic or local practitioner to lead a group discussion.

■ Some different key themes are suggested. You might choose to spend 15 – 20 minutes on each area, or decide to focus the whole discussion on one of the issues for a more detailed discussion.

A discussion could address some or all of the following questions:

- To what extent do you feel **Labour lost economic credibility** and why? How can it recover?

- How can Labour **convince the electorate** that it will spend effectively, not spend excessively, but still spend where necessary?

- How much tax is it fair for people on **middle incomes** to pay?

- How can Labour avoid being **outflanked** by the Conservatives and Liberal Democrats on tax?

- The author advocates a '**New Economic Fabianism**' which recognises that the economy is dynamic and which is anti-statist, while promoting an important role for the State. What would this look like?

- What should a **reformed City** look like?

Please let us know what you think

Whatever view you take of the issues, we would very much like to hear about your discussion. Please send us a summary of your debate (perhaps 300 words) to debate@fabians.org.uk.

The Solidarity Society

Why we can afford to end poverty, and how to do it with public support.

Tim Horton and James Gregory

This report sets out a strategy for how to reduce, eliminate and prevent poverty in Britain.

'The Solidarity Society' is the final report of a project to commemorate the centenary of Beatrice Webb's 1909 Minority Report of the Royal Commission on the Poor Law. It addresses how the values and insights of the Minority Report can animate and inspire a radical contemporary vision to fight and prevent poverty in modern Britain.

The report makes immediate proposals to help build momentum for deeper change. It also seeks to learn lessons from the successes and failures of post-war welfare history, as well as from international evidence on poverty prevention.

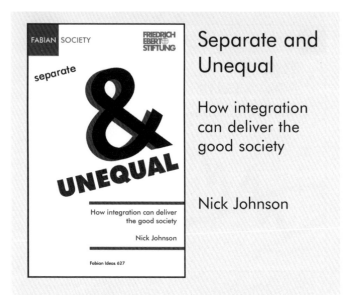

Separate and Unequal

How integration can deliver the good society

Nick Johnson

Britain is separate because it is unequal, and it is unequal because it is separate.

The gap between rich and poor, having exploded during the 1980s, is still growing, despite measures to address poverty in the 13 years of Labour Government. At the same time, we face growing fragmentation in our communities.

In this Fabian Ideas pamphlet, Nick Johnson argues that the politics of integration and equality have become fractured and that we can make the clearest case for both by showing what integration really means.

The effect that a more integrated society would have on all our lives will be a powerful message for progressive politicians: equality and integration must live together or fall apart.

JOIN THE FABIANS TODAY
Join us and receive at least four pamphlets or
books a year as well as our quarterly magazine,
'Fabian Review'.

I'd like to become a Fabian for just £9.95

I understand that should at any time during my six-month introductory
membership period I wish to cancel, I will receive a refund and keep all
publications received without obligation. After six months I understand my
membership will revert to the annual rate as published in *Fabian Review*,
currently £35 (ordinary) or £18 (unwaged) by Direct Debit.

Name	Date of birth
Address	
	Postcode
Email	
Telephone	

Instruction to Bank   Originator's ID: 971666

Bank/building society name	
Address	
	Postcode
Acct holder(s)	
Acct no.	Sort code

DIRECT Debit

I instruct you to pay direct debits from my account at the request of the
Fabian Society. The instruction is subject to the safeguards of the Direct Debit
Guarantee.

Signature	Date

Return to:
Fabian Society Membership
FREEPOST SW 1570
11 Dartmouth Street, London SW1H 9BN